A Bloody
Picnic

A Bloody Picnic

TOMMY'S HUMOUR, 1914–18

ALAN WEEKS

Cover illustrations: Both images (front and back) are cartoons by Bruce Bairnsfather, courtesy of the Holts; originally in black and white, coloured for cover illustration purposes only

First published 2010

The History Press
The Mill, Brimscombe Port
Stroud, Gloucestershire, GL5 2QG
www.thehistorypress.co.uk

British Library Cataloguing in Publication Data.
A catalogue record for this book is available from the British
Library.

ISBN 978 0 7524 5668 3

Typesetting and origination by The History Press
Printed in Great Britain

Contents

Do you Suffer From Cheerfulness?

Cheerful on the Somme

When the horrific Battle of the Somme had been raging for a month, the trench journal *The Somme Times*, of 31 July 1916, posed the question: 'Do you suffer from cheerfulness?'

Private Hudson, a veteran of the Lancashire Regiment, appeared to have this painful condition. Whilst on sentry duty, looking over the trench parapet during this fateful month of July 1916, Hudson was struck on the leg by a shell splinter but remained serenely at his post and even started to sing:

> Ai love the ladies,
> Ai love to be amongst the girls.

Not many days later a gas shell hit the parapet a few inches from Corporal Baker's head. 'Give me a proper 'eadache that 'as, sir, give you me word on it, sir,' he commented breezily to Captain Charles Edmonds.

Not far away on the same day, 'Spider' Webb from Stepney was standing with two chums on the duckboards at the bottom of their trench when a shell landed at their feet. Spider's comrades were killed instantly and one of his legs was blown away from the knee. 'What's happened, Webb?' called an officer frantically.

Now Private Webb was a good cricketer. 'Blimey, what's happened, sir,' he responded cheerfully, 'is one over, two bowled.' Then he glanced down at the mess where he once had a leg. 'And I'm stumped, sir.' Only then did he collapse into a faint.

Two 'Leeds Pals' (the 15th Battalion of the West Yorkshire Regiment, or 15/West Yorkshires) were among the 30–40,000 wounded on the first day of the Battle of the Somme (the 'Black Day' of the British Army during which another 20,000 or so were killed). At least these two were able to walk back to the field dressing station. They were directed to the 'Elephant', a round, corrugated structure.

'Come on, Jack,' said one, half-carrying his pal. 'This way to the Elephant and Castle. They might even pull us a pint, mate.'

Jolly Officers

Cheerfulness was not confined to other ranks on that day (or any day). The commanding officer of the 1/Hampshires, mortally wounded and lying half-submerged at the bottom of a shell hole, offered advice to the private next to him, who could still move: 'Well, if you knows of a better 'ole,' he said, mimicking the caption on perhaps the most famous cartoon of the war (drawn by Captain Bruce Bairnsfather), 'go to it.'

John Glubb (7th Field Company, Royal Engineers) recalled that during a severe enemy bombardment at Wancourt during the Battle of Arras (24 April 1917) an RE officer from another field company was desperately trying to get back to his own unit and was in grave danger in the open fields. He arrived breathlessly in Glubb's ditch and asked if there was a regular interval between each explosion.

'Three minutes,' said Glubb.

So his visitor waited for the next crump and then prepared to make a headlong dash for it.

'Well, tempus fugit, old boy, as the Chinaman say. Bye, bye,' was his jolly parting shot.

Alfred McLelland Burrage of the Artists' Rifles met a similar situation near Ytres during the massive German offensive of March

1918. He was in a sunken road and a platoon came scampering down a bank on to it, trying to take cover from a hail of shells. However, there was little similarity in the speech and demeanour of the officer compared to the one at Wancourt. He was shaking like a leaf and urinated in the road and passed wind vociferously from both ends.

'Them bleedin' shells don't 'arf put the f***ing wind up me,' he confessed to Burrage. He then issued orders to his men. 'Git orf dahn this bleedin' road in twos and threes. Let's git aht of this bleedin' place.'

So saying, he rapidly led the way up the road. He was, as Charles Edmonds would have described him, an example of the 'urban soldier', a typical Kitchener or New Army officer. These men, recruited as the old British Expeditionary Force (BEF) was decimated in 1914, came from many walks of life, very often holding positions of responsibility in civilian life – managers, supervisors, foremen, professional men, etc.

Edmonds served with a fellow subaltern whom he rated a perfect example of this urban soldier, possessing a 'street arab' sort of humour. This was Lieutenant Marriot, who maintained a flowing babble of silly little jokes and anecdotes unless he was asleep. He seized upon the slightest excuse to be amusing. It helped him to forget the open door of the dugout and what might come through it at any moment.

Captain Sidney Rogerson, travelling in a lorry to Amiens for a break in 1917, had only one companion, whom he called 'B'. 'B' was gallant, floridly handsome, devil-may-care and a great womaniser. This officer's 'conversation' during the journey consisted of a monologue about how drunk he was going to get in Amiens. 'Solid ivory from the neck up', was Rogerson's verdict. But 'B' was undoubtedly cheerful if nothing much else.

Captain Tom Adlam (7/Beds and Herts), who was awarded a VC for his bravery during the Battle of the Somme, also kept up a steady stream of crude comments and dirty jokes and stories. 'Who's farted?' was his catchphrase.

Trying to be Cheerful

Edmonds reckoned that cheerfulness reached 'hysterical' proportions as men were preparing to leave the comparative safety of the trench to venture into no-man's-land, even just on night patrols. Trench 'cheerfulness', according to George Coppard (2/Queen's Royal West Surreys, or just Queen's for short), was not the same as the relaxed merriment of civilian life.

The soldiers tried to be cheerful in their letters home (more examples are shown in Chapter Ten), hoping to reassure their folks that they were 'quite well', as the official army postcards put it. These efforts may not always have been entirely successful, as you can see from the following example sent by a lance corporal in Robert Graves' Company early in 1915:

> Dear Auntie,
> This leaves me in the pink. We are at present wading up to our necks in blood. Send me fags and a life-belt. This war is a booger,
> Love and kisses.

". . . while I got their ' harness ' they can't get up to any mischief."

Published by kind permission of the family of Bert Thomas.

They didn't laugh at anything. Graves noted that the rough-tough and habitually callous ex-Welsh coalminers of the 2/Royal Welch Fusiliers (or 2/RWF) saw nothing amusing in the spectacle of a comrade taking three hours to die after having the top part of his head blown off by a bullet fired from 20 metres away.

Indeed, persistent cheerfulness became more difficult as the war dragged on. Charles Carrington (alias Charles Edmonds) remarked that the inclination of officers in 1914, 1915 and 1916 to go 'over the top' (or 'over the bags' or 'over the plonk') into no-man's-land kicking footballs (famously like Captain Billie Nevill on the first day of the Somme) or blowing horns, had evaporated by the end of 1916.

Tommy began to wonder if the war would go on forever – a depressing thought. A divisional follies show in 1917 featured a sketch entitled 'The Trench 1950'. In it a fed-up Tommy and a fed-up Jerry stared at one another from their respective trenches separated by a no-man's-land of about 6 feet. Major Pilditch recalled that he found this the most amusing entertainment he saw during the whole war.

Ironic

The humour could be powerfully ironic, and not only from officers or educated other ranks. The survivors of the 10/Durham Light Infantry (or 10/DLI), reeling away from the dreadful Battle of Delville Wood, Somme (16 September 1916), had lost the majority of their comrades. As they staggered back to rest they were passed by a battalion who still had shiny buttons and some enthusiasm for the battle ahead. But catching sight of the Durhams wiped the smiles off their faces. 'What's it like up there, chum?' one asked, somewhat anxiously.

'A bloody picnic,' came the grim reply. The Durhams trudged on.

Captain Julian Grenfell (1/Royal Dragoon Guards) was one of the small, original BEF which crossed the English Channel in August 1914, looking forward to the fun of teaching the Hun a painful lesson. 'A picnic with a purpose' was the way Grenfell looked at it. He belonged, like most of his fellow officers, to an Edwardian social class who enjoyed picnics. But it was doubtful whether any of the

"Arf a Mo, Kaiser.' – "Arf a Mo' was, in fact, a brand of fag which, according to many Tommies, tasted of seaweed. Drawing by Bert Thomas. Published by kind permission of the family of Bert Thomas.

10/DLI had ever supped an 'Edwardian Champagne Cup' at a country picnic. But at least one of them was a master of irony.

There must have been many encounters like this one. On the 'Black Day' the South Staffordshires, having suffered catastrophic losses, were just as shabby, dirty, hollow-eyed and grime-streaked as the Durhams later at Delville Wood. A staff corporal had his version of the events of the day which he generously shared with passing units: 'General F***-up was in command again!' he informed them merrily.

Dislocation

Volunteer soldiers of working-class origin did not find it difficult to be disdainful about those who had sent them to this bloody war. Similar dislocation existed between officers and men who spent a lot of time on the front line and senior officers ('Brass Hats') who seldom appeared in it (also see Chapter Four).

Moreover, the real 'Western Front' often wondered if the 'Home Front' had any idea how horrific the front line was or whether they cared to know. Sarcasm reached new heights with this possibility. Early in 1915 a company commander of the Argyll and Sutherland Highlanders spent some leave in London. On his return to France he was quizzed by fellow officers about the main concerns in the capital. He reported that the overriding topic of conversation was the latest Charlie Chaplin film.

'I was a bit anxious about things at home,' reflected Major 'Kemp' (not his real name), the CO of this battalion, in response to this revelation. 'But I see now there is nothing to worry about. It's a great country. We shall win all right.'

Indeed, the advice from England to the boys on the front line at this stage of the war was 'keep your heads up'. However, Private Bernard Livermore (2/20 Londons), known popularly as 'Long 'Un', was constantly advised in the trenches to 'keep his head down'. All a German sniper needed was a four-second view of a potential victim.

In the Livermore case, a visiting (briefly) brigadier commented to the Londoner's CO: 'Man's too tall for the trench.' But Bernard's rosy vision of a cushy job at Brigade HQ never materialised. Moreover, he didn't even get the false teeth he had been promised to replace those molars knocked out by Huntley & Palmer's No 4 'dog biscuits', one of the mainstays of Tommy's diet.

Help from Home

Of course, families and friends in Britain were terrified at the prospect of their loved ones being killed or wounded. Londoners turned out in their thousands to greet the hospital trains coming into Waterloo and Victoria, and threw flowers over their heroes. Millions of parcels were dispatched across the Channel to France and Flanders. Helpful ideas flowed across, too. Andrew Clark, Rector of Great Leighs in Essex, wrote to Lord Kitchener (26 January 1915) proposing the use of fishing tackle to send messages from the support trenches to the front trenches. Bigger and stouter reels and rods could be used to bring up supplies from the dumps. Kitchener's office thanked Clark for his contribution to the war effort.

Horatio Bottomley, a well-known journalist, visited the Gavrelle front near Arras in September 1917, in preparation for one of his propaganda articles – 'Somewhere in Hell: What I have seen. What I have done.' This was some event: war correspondents in the trenches were rarer than generals and there had been calls for a new military medal – 'For Distinguished Lying off the Field'.

On hearing of Bottomley's imminent presence, the cinema sergeant of the 15th Highland Division asked Colonel Nicholson if he should 'Get my gun, if I can find it'. Gavrelle Switch was 4,000 yards behind the front line and never under fire.

'Stand on the fire step, Mr Bottomley, and you will see,' invited the colonel, but the little man crouched nervously down in the bottom of the trench. However, he managed to raise himself a little for the official photographs, demanding that the caption for them indicate that they were taken a hundred yards from the enemy. They put him in a gas mask for one of the pictures and Colonel Nicholson was hoping that the little brute would suffocate (see illustration).

Horatio Bottomley, the journalist, tries on a gas mask.

The Mudhook, the Royal Naval Division trench newspaper, celebrated Bottomley's visit and subsequent article, and suggested that they would inspire the troops to even greater efforts. In the meantime, *The Mudhook* wondered what steps were being taken to ameliorate the hacking coughs of our gallant soldiers. Brigadiers were sitting huddled over some distant fires drinking bottles of wine to soothe their lacerated throats. Young officers with a passion for oatmeal biscuits were being denied this delight. Bottomley was beseeched to send cough drops to alleviate all this suffering.

Bottomley was at work again in the *John Bull* magazine in November 1917, at a time when the Battle of Passchendaele (or Third Ypres) had more or less ground to a halt in the thick Flanders mud. His article was called 'Non-stop to Berlin', another supreme example of his journalistic craft.

The officers of the 2/West Yorkshires at Citadel Camp had just digested Bottomley's latest offering when orders from Divisional HQ listed extra items to be carried up to the front by all men. Tommy already resembled a 'Christmas tree' when stumbling in the slime up dark communication trenches. Now, in addition to the existing heavy load, he had to lug as many trench boards as possible, plus extra picks, shovels, wire and screw pickets, and a large bottle of whale oil for their feet – apparently, according to Horatio Bottomley, all the way to Berlin.

In 1922 Horatio Bottomley, MP was imprisoned for fraud in connection with post-war Victory Bonds.

There were other interesting publications in *John Bull*. In 1916, before the Battle of the Somme, it predicted rapid and total victory. As a result, in 1917, with no end of the war in sight, there was a popular poem which went round the trenches:

> We always keep our copies by
> And that is why we prophesy,
> The war was over last July,
> It said so in *John Bull*.

Cuckoos Along the Menin Road

But wartime irony reached its most sublime levels in probably the most famous trench journal, *The Wipers Times* (and its various successors). The editors of this classic satire were Captain (later Lieutenant-Colonel) F.J. ('Fred') Roberts and Lieutenant (later Major) J.H. Pearson. They wrote or stage-managed irony of quality, based on dislocation with the Home Front, often expressed, when you consider the precarious situation these officers and their comrades found themselves in, via a painful but very comic nostalgia for home (there is more *Wipers Times* in Chapter Three).

In the first issue (12 February 1916), a 'correspondent' signing himself as 'A Lover of Nature' claimed to have heard the first cuckoo of spring along the Menin Road. This well-known thoroughfare ran east out of Ypres and had been the focus of two prolonged and fierce battles in 1914 and 1915, and would be at the centre of an even larger and bloodier confrontation in 1917.

In the second issue of the journal (26 February 1916), 'One Who Knows' disputed the claim made by 'A Lover of Nature'. 'One Who Knows' had heard a cuckoo along the Menin Road at least two days before 'A Lover of Nature'. He went on to accuse 'A Lover of Nature' of knowing nothing about 'Nature'. What this twerp had heard in all probability along the Menin Road was a sniper calling to its mate.

The conflict broadened. On 6 March 'A Lover of Nature' hit back at the slurs on his reputation from this 'scurrilous, lying effusion' called 'One Who Knows'. He resented this other's claim to be the first in 1916 to hear the cuckoo along the Menin Road.

Another 'correspondent' – 'A Nocturnal Prowler' – joined in by asserting that he had heard a nightingale along the Menin Road, but yet another – 'Fed-up' – ended this vituperous exchange by condemning the waste of valuable space taken up by the cuckoo (and the nightingale) in such a renowned journal. Actually, Captain Roger Pocock of the 178 Labour Company did hear the song of a skylark one night at the time of year when this was impossible, at least, according to 'Nature'. Staring into the gloom he discerned one of his men perched on top of a wagon imitating the bird. He could also do crows and tits.

What Were They Laughing At?

In October 1917 the 16/Sherwood Foresters were wallowing in a vast expanse of liquid mud in the Passchendaele battlefield near Kitchener Wood. The ground was totally pitted with shell holes and they were filled with water to varying depths. The trick, in order to move forwards or backwards, was to ascertain the depth of the water in front of you or behind. If you lost your footing you were in trouble.

The padre of the Foresters had stayed with them throughout the battle. He was the Rev. John Bloxam and it was he who fell headlong into the water. Fortunately, it was only a couple of feet deep and so the Foresters scrambled down to get him out. But, try as hard as they could, these brawny men could not shift Bloxam out of the morass. He was completely wedged in the glue. He looked at them in despair but, suddenly, he started to laugh uproariously. It was infectious: the Foresters lay back in the water and laughed their heads off, perhaps because they felt helpless. Even a passing stretcher party stopped to have a laugh, including the poor sod on the stretcher.

The story had a happy ending: they managed to get him out – soggy and plastered with mud and still laughing.

Jerry was shelling the Royal Horse Artillery from Hill 60 in the Ypres Salient in the summer of 1915. A shell fell on the dugout where a major was sleeping on a bunk. He was buried up to his neck in rain-sodden soil. He became dimly aware of the heavy weight on his chest but he was a very tired man.

'How dreadful,' he muttered and promptly went back to sleep.

A few moments later, 2nd Lieutenant Julian Tyndale-Biscoe went to the dugout. All he could see was his major's head sticking out of the slime. He awoke him by tapping his face. They stared at one another and then burst into hysterical mirth. They got him out, too.

Corporal James Brown-Gingell of the Royal Engineers led a group of men back along a communication trench called 'Lovers' Walk', carrying heavy bags of food in pitch darkness. Enemy shells were raining down around them. This ration party had to keep close together in case they got lost and so, when Brown-Gingell slipped and fell into the water at the bottom of the trench, all the men following him fell down as well like a pack of cards. As they squirmed about in the mud trying to disentangle themselves someone started roaring and shaking with laughter and that was it: they all joined in. Perhaps it was because the trench was called 'Lovers' Walk'.

Medical officers had a perennial problem trying to find suitable places for their front-line aid posts. They had to be near enough to the trenches to do their work and so were vulnerable to enemy fire. The MO of the 2/RWF thought he had cracked it when he discovered a miraculously unscathed two-storey building on the edge of the village of Cuinchy during the run-up to the Battle of Loos in September 1915. However, the drawback of using a two-storey building was that the top half might fall down on the lower half if the house was struck by a shell.

This was exactly what happened on 23 September. Several medical orderlies came cascading down with the ceiling on to wounded men lying on stretchers. Luckily, no one was seriously hurt and, moreover, everybody found it ludicrously funny.

On 27 February 1917 Armentières suffered one of its periodic heavy enemy bombardments. The road where John Reith was billeted was particularly badly hit. He rushed out into the street in his pyjamas. His groom stared out of an upstairs window, still half-asleep but with a broad grin on his face. He was covered in ceiling plaster: the ceiling had fallen on him. He regarded it as hilarious. 'He was seeing something funny in it. And it was funny,' wrote Reith later.

However, most of Tommy's humour was pretty straightforward. There were just soldiers who constantly amused their chums. The war had only just begun when Billy and his mates of the 2nd Battalion, Royal Welch Fusiliers (2/RWF) arrived in Rouen on 10 August. They made straight for an *estaminet* and Billy ordered wine in a mixture of English, Hindustani, Chinese and an obscene French word which he had learned already.

The proprietor gave a Gallic shrug, pretending not to understand anything and Billy repeated the French word he had learned. His view of foreigners was that they all needed a good bashing. Such a threat produced a bottle of red wine, vintage unknown.

Our next view of Billy is a couple of months later, riding up the Champs Elysée in a nice carriage and in the company of two of these 'foreigners' – of the young and female type.

TWO

Comic Cuts

In the Dark

There was no shortage of comedy and comedians in the trenches at night. Near Gavrelle in the summer of 1917 an officer was trying to locate a company of the Artists' Rifles. You couldn't see your hand in front of your face. 'Are you an Artist?' he asked a dim shape.

The 'dim shape' in question was a member of the Drake Battalion, not known for polite conversation. 'No, I'm a f***ing comedian,' it responded crisply.

Lieutenant Blake of the Royal Fusiliers, running desperately along a trench seeking help for his men after a shell had struck the parapet, called into the dark interior of a dugout: 'Where's the company commander?'

'If I knoo,' came a thundering voice from the darkness, 'I'd shoot the barstard!'

Major Frank Crozier commanded a battalion of the Royal Irish Rifles and was going up to the front on a dark night early in 1915 and was in grave danger of falling down one of the myriad holes in the trenches and getting more soaked than he already was – or drowned. Apart from Very Lights going off every few minutes there was no illumination. Crozier's orderly lit a torch.

'Put out that f***ing light,' growled a nearby sentry, 'you f***ing c*** – do you want us all shot up?'

'Sorry,' Crozier replied, 'but you know where you are and I'm damned if I know where I am and I'd rather be shot than drowned any night.'

Corporal Robinson, known as 'Buggy', was a New Zealander in the 2/RWF and he was famous for all sorts of antics, one of which was running up and down the trench on the bitterly cold nights of winter 1914–15, shouting, 'Shoo! Shoo! Look out, I'm an express train!' We'll meet him again.

Slapstick

During the day pure slapstick was more possible. Private M'Leary's (Argyll and Sutherland Highlanders) contribution consisted of donning his gas helmet and pretending to drink his tea through it. Private Darrell's party piece was more elaborate and usually in evidence during enemy bombardments, such as that inflicted by howitzers at Bois Grenier on 30 January 1915. He unfurled a battered and torn umbrella (it was also raining) and cried out for succour from St Mungo, a Glaswegian saint, before collapsing in a crumpled heap on the duckboards, legs kicking wildly in all directions. It made him feel better and his mates were used to it, and it did take their minds off the hails of metallic death coming their way – for a minute or two, anyway.

When he was a captain in the 2/Cameron Highlanders, James Jack (see also Chapter Three) was somewhat alarmed during the Battle of Loos (26 September 1915) to be confronted by an exuberant Highlander juggling with three live grenades and occasionally dropping one. Captain Jack, in his inimitable way, wondered whether the juggler could desist until his juggling skills improved. However, the Scot pointed out, with respect sir, that they wouldn't unless he practised.

Callous

Tommy's attempts at humour were sometimes callous. The 1/Hull Pals arrived from another theatre of war in the spring of 1916 and settled on the front at Beaumont Hamel in the Somme sector. On 29 March they suffered their first fatality on the Western Front. He was Private Stanley Horsfall, who happened to be the battalion's goalkeeper. 'He has stopped one at last,' commented a 'Pal'.

Such jokes were also directed at NCOs, officers, commanding officers and certainly at 'Brass Hats', whose work usually took them well away from the front line. Indeed, no one was spared. A friend said to Private Maxwell, 'Kitchener will go down in history as one of our greatest soldiers.'

'He's gone down already,' Maxwell pointed out, referring to the sinking of HMS *Hampshire* off the Orkneys, in June 1916 en route to Russia, with the loss of nearly all hands, including Lord Kitchener and his entire staff.

George Coppard, then in the 37 Machine Gun Company, recalled a hapless, 'middle-aged' 2nd lieutenant who was visibly terrified by enemy fire and rendered useless by it. He was also disfigured by a hump on his back (July 1917). 'Why don't you put that little bleeder down and give him a walk,' someone suggested from a distance at dusk.

Private Joe Yarwood of the 94 Field Ambulance was up with the artillery on 28 June 1916 as the British bombardment and the enemy counter-bombardment, which preceded the Battle of the Somme, were in full swing. He was dutifully tending wounded men and was in great danger himself. But he was blessed with a less-than-kind section corporal. The medical orderlies used blankets to sow up around corpses. At one point the sneering, foul-mouthed corporal remarked: 'You – you long bugger – if one hits you you'll need more than one bloody blanket.'

Joe didn't think that was very funny but he kept the corporal amused because every time the British guns fired, his helmet fell down over his face.

Something similar happened to Private Douglas Roberts (7/East Kents). He was one of a ration party carrying up heavy loads along a communication trench. He was already loaded up with a 2-gallon can of water, three Lewis gun panniers and some mortar ammunition. 'Give that big barstard some more gear,' shouted his sergeant. 'Here, catch hold of this sack of bread, you f***ing gorilla.'

Wit?

But the rather more reflective soldiers of the 2/RWF seemed to have a more ethereal humour. They imagined the souls of those killed on the Western Front looking down on them and dancing a two-step and clicking their heels together in 'holy glee' that they were out of it.

The 'Old Soldier' ruminated on the mystery of appeals from the clergy of both combatants to bring down His wrath on the other side. 'God's truth!' he exclaimed. 'That poor old chap above must be nearly bald-headed through scratching his poll, trying to answer the prayers of both sides.' Other 'old soldiers' derided newcomers in various ways but always opening with the phrase 'I was here before your ...' Examples included 'before your ballacks dropped' and 'before you lost the cradle marks on your arse'.

During the Battle of Poelcappelle in the Ypres Salient in 1917, the Cyclist Battalion of the XVIII Corps held aloft lifelike dummy Tommies on poles, worked by strings. The cunning plan was to convince Jerry that an attack was imminent. It was a 'Chinese attack': the real attack was planned for somewhere else. The dummies got an absolute pasting. 'Them dummies is having a really rough time,' observed Private V.R. Magill, as his puppet finally gave up the ghost.

An officer riding behind the parados of a busy trench was mortified when his steed urinated on the men below. He offered profuse apologies, but a soldier responded: 'Never mind, sir, it could have been your horse.'

Corpse Humour

They were surrounded by death in the trenches. Corpses stuck out of trench walls, parapets and paradoses where they had been constructed near disused trenches or on former battle zones. Exploding shells could throw up even more of these horrors. When a brigadier visited the 2/Leinsters during heavy fighting in the Ypres Salient in 1915 he complained to Captain F.C. Hitchcock about the leg of a German corpse protruding from the parapet. Private Finnegan was ordered to remove it. But digging out the offending limb would have entailed dismantling and restoring a section of the parapet, so Private Finnegan hacked off the leg with a shovel. He was not a happy man. 'And what the bloody hell will I hang me equipment on now?' he demanded in exasperation to no one in particular.

When the 1/Herts took over a trench near Thiepval on the Somme it was full of corpses, which had been there for some time. They were bloated with gas; one lay right across the bottom of the trench and was not easily avoided and every time a 1/Herts trod on his chest, his tongue popped out. It never ceased to amuse them.

Corpses of British soldiers were not necessarily treated with any greater respect. Joe Yarwood remembered that he and his mates continually walked on the top of a head sticking out of the mud and daily checked on how bald it was getting.

A letter from Mildred, daughter of the Rev. Andrew Clark of Great Leighs, recounted an event described to her by a soldier on leave. Two men of a Scots regiment were shovelling earth on German 'corpses' when one of them came to and started screaming, 'Me no deaded! Me no deaded!' They stared at him dispassionately. 'Agh!' cried one in disdain. 'Shove some earth on him, Geordie. Them Germans are such liars that no one can believe a word they say.'

After the Battle of Loos in September 1915, 2nd Lieutenant Norman Dillon of the Northumberland Fusiliers watched two of his men trying to remove German corpses from a trench they wanted to occupy. They were not totally devoid of humanity: some of the bodies were decapitated and they were trying to put the right head with the right body. They were rolling the heads about like footballs. 'Get hold of this one, Bill, and see if it fits any of yours,' called one of them.

The 10/Essex had a leg in a trench wall adorned in a green, expensive-looking, silk sock. 'What a toff!' reckoned an Essex Tommy.

In March 1916 the 2/RWF in the Cambrai line had a pulpy German arm to contend with. But the dreadful arm still sported an expensive watch and the Fusiliers liked to keep it wound up – and then someone pinched it.

It was even possible to use humour for a comrade just killed, but not, of course, when they were close pals, members of 'household groups', when there was genuine grief at the loss. An 'elderly' (perhaps 40) latrine attendant of the Welsh Regiment was hit in the latrine trench as he buried excrement. One of the arms of the dead man stretched out on to the duckboards of the main trench. 'Out of the way, you old barstard!' merrily quipped former comrades as they stepped over the arm; or they shook hands with it and said, 'Put it there, Billy boy.' (Perhaps it was the way tough ex-miners expressed their grief.)

Toilet Humour

Latrines were vulnerable to enemy fire because the accesses to them usually ran at right angles to the main trench. Soldiers thus made their visits to the facilities as brief as possible, also hastened by the pong. The urgency was greater during shelling, including gas attacks. If you were sat there and the gas alarm rang out (hanging empty shell cases struck with a trenching tool), there was a real dilemma. Should you finish the job and pull up your trousers or put on your gas mask first? Sometimes there was not time for both operations. As early as April 1915 the 2/RWF replaced rear latrines with buckets in the trench. These were emptied at night into convenient shell holes as far from the trench as possible. It was a matter of debate amongst the soldiers as to the safest and most convenient system.

Squatters in the karsy were also at risk from their own artillery. 'Dave Barney' of the Artists' Rifles was sitting in a latrine in the Gavrelle trenches in the summer of 1917 when it was struck by an 18-pounder from behind. Dave was a stretcher-bearer and was lucky not to have been carried off on one of his own stretchers. But he remained as cheerful, chirpy and Cockney as ever. 'Never,' he claimed, 'were there such times for the working classes.' He probably hadn't been on any pre-war picnics either, although he was fond of Epping Forest and irony.

When a similar event struck Private Stearsby (although at least it was an enemy whizz-bang) of the 7/Royal Warwickshires under Messines Ridge (April 1915), he went missing. Anxious pals were very relieved when he appeared from the smoke with his habitual .

grin and comment: 'It's them Number Nines the Pox Doctor gave me,' he explained, and his mates had a very good laugh because the 'Pox Doctor' was standing right next to them. 'Number Nines' were the classic remedy for constipation, although that condition could be less dangerous in trenches.

Lieutenant Ellison of the Royal Horse Artillery was sitting in the (grander) officer's latrine (supplied with toilet paper depicting the kaiser) in April 1916 when a direct hit shattered the whole structure, totally exposing him. But he was unhurt and calm. 'That was good,' he called to anxious fellow officers as he sat there. 'I was feeling rather constipated until that came along.'

Friendly Fire

Whilst on the subject of friendly fire, on the first day of the Battle of Arras (9 April 1917), the 1/East Yorkshires were caught in a bombardment on open land. 'It's okay,' called out one to his mates, 'they're ours.' He could have been serious.

Sergeant Priestley had a different take on friendly fire whilst sheltering from it in a shell hole with his lieutenant. 'Tell you what, sir,' he observed, 'the blokes that's firing them guns must be conscientious objectors on a recruit's course.'

'Where's that one going?'
Drawing by Henry Ogle.

In February 1915 an artillery battery behind the 2/RWF was trying to establish range and direction. Four trial shots were carried out: the first fell in no-man's-land, the second on the Fusiliers' parapet, the third just behind their parados and the fourth on to Company HQ.

The gunners phoned the infantry: 'Is that enough?' they enquired.

Humour Across No-Man's-Land

Unlucky Tommies could be stuck out in no-man's-land after tricky night patrols which could take them right up to the enemy wire or even beyond if a raid was planned. Private Davenport of the 10/South Wales Borderers always urinated on the enemy wire, a sort of visiting card – 'Davenport woz 'ere', sort of thing.

But you could finish up in a shell hole with a German corpse. 'Heavens,' moaned one such unfortunate Tommy, 'have I got to spend the night with you?'

Corporal Robinson, or 'Buggy', of the 2/RWF, whom we met earlier in the chapter, was an enthusiastic souvenir-hunter in no-man's-land at night. His CO turned a blind eye to this hobby, although he did warn Buggy he was on his own if he got into trouble. Buggy was stranded out in a hole one night with two German corpses. Being a great talker, he told all his mates about it when he safely returned the next morning.

He was out again on the following night. 'Here,' he told all and sundry on his return, 'you know I said there were two stiffs in the hole, well, there wasn't, see. There was only one Jerry, only his head was on one side of the hole and his body was on the other. I like to get things right, see.'

On 17 July 1916, on the Somme battlefield, a member of the 56th Division was actually out there for three successive nights and days. On his return he was quizzed by his platoon officer on why he had been forced to stay out for so long. 'Well, sir,' came the explanation, 'on the first night I was afraid Fritz might spot me.'

'And the second night?'

'I was pretty near our wire, sir, and I was afraid that you would mistake me for Fritz and shoot me.'

'But why come in now – the Germans are still there and so are we?'

'It started to rain, sir.'

Small-scale, unofficial truces were possible out there. An officer of the 2/Leinsters spotted a private chatting with a German at the bottom of a large crater (St Eloi, 1915). They were discussing rank: Jerry said he was a corporal and Private Bates said he was a company sergeant-major.

All sorts of 'live and let live' situations (see Chapter Thirteen for more) existed on the Western Front, perhaps to a lesser extent after 1915. This is sometimes categorised as 'ritualisation', e.g. only sending over shells at 'agreed' times and at 'agreed' targets or shooting inaccurately on purpose. Officers still had to submit reports:

> *Twelve little Willies at noon to the tick.*
> *Get our heads down and got them down quick.*
> *Peaceful and calm the rest of the day.*
> *Nobody hurt and nothing to pay.*

(Report from an officer in the 1/Queen's
Westminster Rifles, September 1915, near Ypres)

Ritualisation also included 'machine gun music'. Practitioners could loose off to the tune of a well-known song – 'Dum, der, der, dum, dum', and both sides could add, 'Bang! Bang!' German experts in this art were granted nicknames by the 41st Division, such as 'Duckboard Dick', 'Peter the Painter', 'Parapet Joe' and, everyone's favourite, 'Happy Harry', who was the star at Ploegsteert ('Plugstreet') Wood in April 1916.

The 7/Royal Sussex had a catapult which could toss a large bully beef tin 90 yards into a German trench (September 1915, near Houplines). Troops of the 5th Division had a piano in a front-line trench in July 1915 and the 10/East Yorkshires had one in the Nieppe Forest sector in July 1918. In both cases the Germans enjoyed listening to the music drifting across no-man's-land and nothing would induce them to fire anywhere near the source of it.

More no-man's-land rhapsody was provided by the wind blowing through empty tins stuck on the wire. According to Henry Ogle of the 7/Royal Warwickshires, the Germans also tied little bells on to the wire for harmony.

Personality

There was a vast range of personalities on the front line. Private Burford of the Welsh Regiment, it was rumoured, was 63 years of age and had last fired a gun in anger in Egypt in 1882. He had been considered too old to take part in the Boer War (1899–1902). In civilian life he was a collier in winter and a tramp in summer.

Colonel Rowland Feilding, CO of the 6/Connaught Rangers, couldn't help noticing the artistic talents of some of his men at Dysart Camp near Ervillers in October 1917. On the projecting foot of a corpse someone had inscribed a calligraphic masterpiece: 'R.I.P.' On a grave there was something more complex – a bas-relief of the head of Christ carved out with a jackknife. Around it was drawn hair and a halo in indelible purple pencil (you had to spit on it to make it work). Feilding didn't know whether to laugh or cry.

With so many exuberant extroverts around, noise levels in the trench could rise despite the danger of a response from Jerry. 'There's too much noise,' complained an NCO of the 4/Black Watch one night. 'Stop your gassing.'

Lance-Corporal Alex Thompson couldn't hear him above the din but did pick up the word 'gas'.

'Quick, boys,' he called, 'Fritz has turned on the gas.'

'Turn on the gas?' echoed a comedian. 'Anyone got a f***ing shilling for the meter?'

Many snatches of intriguing conversations could be picked up. At Berbure, 28 June 1915, when he was a captain in the 3/Coldstream Guards, Rowland Feilding overheard a private (who was obviously depressed) ruefully remark: 'I wish my father had never met my mother.'

There was something of a pause and then a response came: 'Perhaps he didn't.'

Two men were discussing the best ways of dying, also within earshot of Feilding: 'I would rather be killed in a railway accident,' reckoned one of them, 'because you know where you are, but if you are killed by an explosion, where the hell are you?'

Men of the 6/Connaught Rangers were struggling along a communication trench on a wet and very dark night carrying heavy A-shaped pieces of wood which supported the bottom of trenches. 'How do you like being a soldier?' asked one man of his friend, perhaps sarcastically, perhaps philosophically.

'It isn't a soldier you've got to be in this war,' was the bitter reply, 'it's a bloody camel.'

The Coldstream Guards must have been feeling the same when they pinned up a notice, 'Coldstream Guards – Navvies', in their trench.

Often there were practical arrangements to be discussed and, although the Tommies were deadly serious, anyone eavesdropping would be in the same dilemma as Rowland Feilding – not knowing whether to laugh or cry. Men of the Welsh Regiment, by 1918, had developed the practice of pooling their financial resources before an offensive or a raid. The plan was that those who survived would divide the cash equally between them. Those who had been killed would be in no position to complain. The wounded would have escaped, hopefully to Blighty, so would regard the financial loss as worth every penny. Those still in the trench would see their remuneration as well and truly earned.

The CO of a company of the Argyll and Sutherland Highlanders was a character and no mistake. The bane of his life, apart from the Germans, was 'the football team' (sometimes also known as a 'travelling circus'). This was a group of men moving around the trenches and firing off their mortar. However, they were not welcome anywhere because of potential reprisals from German mortars as soon as the football team had departed.

'Take it away!' screamed the major. 'Take your darned liver-pill out of this! Burn it! Bury it! Eat it! But not here! Go away!' ... which, for the Western Front, was quite mild, because it had many ways of telling someone to go away. Rejecting 'football teams' might have been the origin of the NIMBY concept.

Travel Broadens the Mind

Comedy, having arrived in France, followed Tommy on to French trains. Henry Ogle joined one with his battalion on 22 March 1915. It had one proper carriage which was for officers and the rest consisted of open trucks and horse boxes. A pal of Ogle's tried to read what was printed on the sides of the horse boxes. 'Chevorks eight, ommies forty' was the result. ''Ow can they get them all in?'

The 'Leaning Virgin' in Albert. The legend was that when the Madonna and Child fell, the war would end.

'It's "or",' explained Ogle.

'Then why the 'ell can't they write "or", then?'

Horses were led into some of these boxes and the Royal Warwickshires were led into the others. 'I'll bet they've got more straw than us,' declared the expert in French.

Another mate patiently explained the situation. 'You're not going to 'ave the same as an 'orse being as you're an 'uman.'

That was pondered on, but the thoroughly puzzled Tommy returned his attention to the limited accommodation on the train: 'I reckon if forty French get in them they're 'alf-starved little buggers.'

He looked out along the train. ''Ere,' he exclaimed, 'there ain't no engine! There ain't no bloody engine! Come on, Number Twelve Platoon, get out and shove or we'll be late for the war.'

An enormous engine arrived and was greeted with loud cheers. It took them at a lumbering pace to a level crossing and then stopped and issued the tiniest little 'toot! toot!' imaginable. The Warwicks fell about but the driver and fireman, undeterred, waved and shouted, '*À bas les bosches!*'

They got to Winnezeele in Flanders on 23 March. 'Winnie-zeely,' read our linguist. 'We are here! We are where? This ain't any – bloody – where!'

Trains habitually deposited Tommy miles from his billet so he marched to it. Then he usually marched up to the front and away from it (hopefully), apart from the occasional lift. They enjoyed passing other units.

'Well, strike me pink! If it ain't the boys what eats orf plates.'

'Does your mother know you're out?'

'Kind of nasty smell round here, don't you think, Bill?'

Marching infantry passed a signalman up a pole. 'Some say "good old signals".' – 'Others say "f*** old signals".' He tried to ignore them but found it difficult to suppress a grin.

'He's going up the line.'

'Lend 'im your button 'ook.'

The signalman at last came to life. 'Oh, it's the bloody infantry. What you doing up the line, anyway?'

'We're looking for the General Post Office.'

'Well, you've found it.'

'Give me the Ipswich switch, Miss, it's the Ipswich switch which I require.'

The signalman could contain his mirth no longer. 'Silly sods!' he said.

But if it was Private 'Nobby' Clarke from Hammersmith who passed you by there would be something from Shakespeare. He was known as 'The Voice' because it was deep, melodious and melodramatic: 'Sweep on, you fat and greasy citizens!'

Gunner George Cole was marching through Albert with the 3/Northumbrian Royal Field Artillery. The statue of the Madonna and Child was hanging down off the spire of the Basilica at a crazy angle (see illustration), but the Child had not fallen from the hands of the Madonna. Hundreds of thousands of Tommies remembered this famous sight. The statue had been struck by a shell and the legend was that when the Child fell the war would end.

'Let's knock it down, now,' suggested George, 'save a lot of trouble.'

At Rest

Arrival in rest areas was the source of much activity. When the 7/ Royal Warwickshires got to Wulverghem in April 1915, a further move to the front was imminent so nerves were frayed. This was a territorial battalion, which meant that everyone knew everyone else in civvy street. The corpulent CSM immediately fell out with Private Giles and Private Steane – clearly not for the first time. 'There's talking in the ranks on parade,' he rasped. 'That was you, Gulliver Giles!'

'Private Giles to you, you old windbag,' muttered Giles under his breath.

'You're answering you are, are you? Any argufying in the ranks with your seen-ior officer is a crime akin to mutinous conduct. You're on active service now and I can shoot you for mutiny, Private Giles, if I want to.' His walrus moustache bristled with anger.

'You'd never catch me, you fat old sod,' muttered Gulliver.

'Crime that man, Sergeant Palmer!' yelled the sergeant-major. 'Crime Steane, as well. Now get out about your jobs and don't forget you're on active service now and no more argufying!'

Sergeant Palmer licked his purple pencil and produced a little notebook and stood in front of Private Giles. 'Name and number,' he demanded.

'Three-o-three, Fred – bloody – Karno,' replied the mutinous soldier.

In the rest areas medical officers could also have problems, especially if American and newly arrived. 'Dave Barney' of the Artists' Rifles calculated that he had been to the toilet twenty-six times in twenty-four hours. 'Gee,' concluded the medic, 'you must have the "Charley's Aunts".' This was a long-running play in London. Dave was given 'medicine and duty'.

Unfortunately, Dave's pal, Alfred Burrage, had not been primed up as to the actual scale of diarrhoea which was being claimed. He told the MO he had been to the toilet seven times in twenty-four hours. 'Gee, man, you're bound up. I'll give you some Number Nines.'

Billeting officers had the job of finding suitable accommodation for soldiers resting in their area. This task sometimes did not run smoothly. The 7th Field Company of the Royal Engineers arrived at

Exhausted stretcher-bearers grab some sleep, near Arras, 29 August 1918. Reproduced by kind permission of the Imperial War Museum (Q7014).

Morcourt on 6 March 1917 to discover that the 8/DLI were occupying their designated billet – the village school. There were exchanges of points of view between the Engineers and the 'Derr-ems'.

'We don't remember anyone wanting our billet when we were in the trench,' called a sarcastic infantryman.

Yet some of these Engineers had been in the thick of battle since 1914 and some of their work was actually carried out in front of the trenches.

'We didn't have no billets in 1914,' pointed out one of these sappers, an effective way of asking whether any Durhams had been around since 1914.

Village schools sounded like decent accommodation; a loft above a pig sty was different. The farmer might be good enough to clear out the pigs but they left behind a powerful aroma. 'Now we know why we've got respirators,' declared James Campbell of the 6/Cameron Highlanders.

CSM Scott of the 2/West Yorkshires had an interesting theory about French farms following an experience of one in November 1917. He reckoned that they were built by putting up some sticks and throwing mud at them. What clung to the sticks was the farmhouse and what fell off was the midden.

Welcome Hostelries

Once settled in and all chores completed, the troops could ferret around for the best cafes or *estaminets*. There was disappointment in Wieltz, near Ypres, in 1915, when Bruce Bairnsfather's platoon discovered that a shell had fallen on a recommended establishment. One man stood behind the wrecked bar and 'operated' an imaginary handle on an imaginary pump.

'And what's yours, mate?' he politely asked the next 'customer'.

But usually they found a warm and fuggy welcome in these places. Egg and chips was the staple diet, washed down by *vin blanc* – 'plonk'. In one of these places there was a picture on the wall depicting Napoleon's army followed by hordes of shabby women. It was entitled '*Les Vivandières*'. Someone explained what this

'Where did that one go?' Cartoon by Bruce Bairnsfather. Reproduced by kind permission of Tonie and Valmai Holt.

meant to a mate, who observed: 'I always thought they were *hors de combat.*'

After a drink or two the singing could start (see Chapter Ten for some of the songs) and high jinks and japes. One glass of plonk was enough to send one man to sleep, snoring profusely. On these occasions Private Maxwell managed to squeeze a sliver of soap into the slumbering bloke's mouth. As he continued to snore, clouds of large, foamy bubbles floated up to the ceiling.

Repartee could be almost surreal – an other ranks' version of 'cuckoos along the Menin Road': 'Cheer up, Parker,' advised Private Drake of the 2/West Yorkshires. 'You look as if you were about to give birth to a baby elephant. What would you do if you suddenly did produce a baby elephant, eh?'

'I'd suckle it,' replied an expressionless Private Parker. In fact, his face never bore any expression.

There were popular stories to tell on these occasions, like the one about a conversation between officers of the Honourable Royal Artillery. One asked the other whether he had paid his subscription and was overheard by an adjacent private who called out in delight to his mates: ''Ere, there's blokes 'ere what have bloody well paid the bloody 'onourable Royal Hartillery to hactually come out 'ere to this bloody country to fight.'

This revelation had been greeted with raucous and prolonged cheering.

Serious Stuff at Rest

There was work to be done in the rest areas, which was sometimes the cause of a lot of grumbling, more training and formal gatherings. Whenever 'The Voice' was present at these meetings, more Shakespeare could be expected. A brigadier was listing all the faults of Nobby Clarke's battalion. 'O, what a world of vile, ill-favoured faults,' intoned Nobby the Shakespearian scholar. On another occasion his own major was preparing to lecture the troops when his chair collapsed and deposited him heavily on the floorboards. 'And when he falls, he falls like Lucifer,' supplied 'The Voice'.

The short silence which followed was punctuated by more of the Bard of Avon: 'A wretched soul, bruised with adversity.' The major, sore bottom and all, shook with laughter.

A lantern slideshow about filling up sandbags was being endured in Cartigny by a captive audience. The captain delivering the address was known as 'The Sandbag King', an enthusiast for filling up sandbags all night in wet and cold trenches. Private Harry was late; he was late because he had come across a crate of champagne in a cellar during excavations to create some gardens in the ruins of this shattered town. Harry staggered into the room and contemplated the scene gravely – the Sandbag King and an audience in a coma of boredom, dreaming of egg and chips. He pointed dramatically at the Sandbag King and in a tone to rival 'The Voice', if not Shakespeare, exclaimed, 'Three f***ing million sandbags', and the audience came back to the land of the living and roared their appreciation.

Games & Tricks

Apart from drinking, eating, singing, etc., Tommies in the rest areas often played indoor games (more 'indoor games' are described in Chapter Eight). For instance, there was 'Housey, Housey' (or 'Bingo') and 'Crown and Anchor'. This was played around a foldable board or roll-up cloth in case the banker had to beat a rapid retreat because the game was banned by the army. The board or cloth was divided into six sections – the Heart, the Crown, the Diamond, the Spade, the Anchor and the Club. The banker had two dice with emblems representing those symbols on the board. Players bet on one or more of the sections and if their emblem showed on the thrown dice they won double their stake.

The owners of these games were real chancers – spivs on the make, able to look after themselves in case of trouble, possibly with the assistance of close friends. As betting proceeded these characters kept up a continual patter:

Here we are again. The Sweaty Socks! Cox and Co., the Army Bankers, badly bent, but never broke, safe as the Bank of England, undefeated because they never fought; the rough and tough, the old and bold! Where you lay we pay. Come and put your money with the little old man. I touch the money, but I never touch the dice. Any more for the lucky old heart? Make it even on the lucky old heart. Are you all done, gentlemen? Are you all done? The diamond, meat-hook, and lucky old sergeant-major [he shakes the dice again]. Now, then, will anyone down on his luck put a little bit of snow on the curse? Does anyone say a bit of snow on the old hook? Has no one thought of the pioneer's tool? Are you all done, gentlemen? Are you all done? Cocked dice are no man's dice. Change your bets or double them. Now, then, up she comes again. The mud-rake, the shamrock, and the lucky old heart. Copper to copper, silver to silver and gold to gold. We shall have to drag the anchor a bit [rattles the dice]. Now who tried his luck on the name of the game?

Lieutenant Edmonds remembered one of these 'Crown and Anchor' gamesters – 'Davey' Jones, a little ex-racecourse tout, a man of unlimited impudence and a singer of scurrilous songs and forever in trouble. His favourite saying was, 'Why the shell ain't made with my name on it'.

Rowland Feilding knew Corporal Pierpoint – clown, buffoon, contortionist and acrobat. At the Divisional Sports Day at Dysert Camp near Ervillers, on 14 October 1917, he walked about on his hands with his legs under his elbows. In the trench he was another one of these experts at gauging where the next shell would fall. Comrades would gather round him and he would send them scurrying to the left or right, or urge them to stay exactly where they were.

Pierpoint also boxed and played in goal at football, keeping up a stream of advice to the referee throughout any game – 'off-side, ref', 'hands, ref', 'that was out, ref' – a sort of Sir Alex Ferguson of the First World War.

'Mr Binks', who belonged to a battalion of the Artists' Rifles, was also a contortionist (he had been on music hall stages) and his favourite trick was saluting officers of other units and then scratching the back of his head with his foot. He was also a latrine orderly and was fond of playing practical jokes on unsuspecting visitors to the rear area. His mates were even quicker out of the karsy than most Tommies. They could never guess what Mr Binks' latest wheeze would be – probably something involving a dead rat.

Jack from Athlone had somehow managed to get himself into the 7/Royal Warwickshires (along with quite a few Londoners). He would come into the crowded *estaminet* (as at Foncquevillers in January 1916) and announce, 'God save all here', and then launch into a tirade against 'authority', his language getting worse and worse until he slumped into a corner and became contrite. 'God forgive me for all these drrr-eadful wor-rrds! And now, for the love of Jesus, have you such a thing as a cigarette about you?'

THREE

Puckish, Wry & Buffalo Bill

James Jack

Major-General R.C. Money, who earlier in his career served under James Jack, described his mentor as 'puckish'. I suppose you could also employ the word 'wry'. Captain Jack arrived with the 1/Cameron Highlanders at Harfleur on 16 August 1914 and remained on the Western Front for the whole war, rising to the rank of general. After the disastrous retreat from Mons, the survivors of the BEF squatted near Paris, and rumours that they would be taken out of the line and refitted and bolstered by units withdrawn from duty around the Empire were welcomed by Jack like all his fellow officers and men. His view of it (recounted in his lively daily diary) was that they should get together with the French and Germans and arrange a seasonal break and come back for a second half – say, in October.

At Harfleur, in August, he was already worried about some of his soldiers because they gave away so many cap badges and tunic buttons as souvenirs to the friendly French citizens. Later, on the retreat from Mons, they lost a lot more equipment and clothing, so Jack was on the lookout for naked Cameronians: there must be some of them about.

The Christmas truces gave him another idea. He suggested that cakes and wine should be taken out to the Germans on nice trays and they should be offered £5 each to surrender. He regarded this as the cheapest way to win the war. He was not wrong there. He also offered

Captain James Jack, 1/Cameron Highlanders, 5 January 1915 (on the right). From the collection of Major-General R.C. Money.

a solution to the very wet weather. The acres of blotting paper which went to waste in HQ offices could be laid down to soak up all the moisture on the Western Front and then transported to Egypt to solve the water shortage there.

The Cameronians sat in the flooded trenches at Bois Grenier in January 1915 and were visited by a colonel. He had only just settled in when a bullet smacked into the parapet inches from his head. The colonel was ready to blame weaknesses in the construction of the parapet, but in Jack's opinion the cause of the near-disaster was the colonel's bald head glinting in the morning sun. It was pouring at the time.

Jack was promoted to major in March 1916, despite such impudence, but not without misgivings on his part because he had sympathy with Siegfried Sassoon's view of majors as 'fierce, bald and short of breath' due to too much port and soft living. In June of that year Jack observed that if ink could win the war then the Allies had a good chance. When he did become a staff officer later in the war, he cut down fiercely on administrative extravagance in his brigade and division.

In November 1916 he was promoted to lieutenant-colonel and became the CO of the 2/West Yorkshires. He had clear opinions about competence and hard work. Whenever he was asked to supply labourers to pioneer companies he always offered A.O.R. (Any Old Rubbish).

Jack had to take his battalion in pursuit of the Germans when they withdrew to the Hindenburg Line in the spring of 1917. Jerry had a nasty habit of leaving booby traps everywhere – in rum jars, stoves, trees, etc. and Jack feared that he could hear ticking in every ruined house.

In 1918 Jack became a brigadier and, despite his desire for good economy, his first order was for a new typewriter because the old one sounded like a tank and mutilated paper. He still insisted on making frequent trips to the trenches. He was in the thick of an enemy bombardment on 2 October 1918, north of Ledeghem, when he noticed a group of men running away and threatened to shoot any man who continued in this direction. In order to emphasise the fact that the shells were going high over their heads, he stood on tiptoe and held his cane high in the air in a comic attempt to reassure the men that they were in no real danger. A sergeant called over, 'You're a topper, sir', a sentiment with which men who served with Jack in two Cameronian battalions, the 2/West Yorkshires and the 27th Brigade, would surely agree.

Captain Billie Nevill

The letters sent home by Captain Billie Nevill of the 8/East Surreys are a skittish delight. On 28 August 1915 he headed up one of these efforts, in a nice send-up of censorship on location – 'Venue, I wonder. Try to guess. Hard to say.' He was writing from a shelter which was 'Jack Johnson proof', 'Jack Johnsons' being large German shells which gave off a lot of black smoke when they exploded (the actual Jack Johnson being the heavyweight boxing champion of the world and black).

In a billet near Albert around the same time Billie described the presence of a 'whopping great' donkey, apparently 'serving a life sentence of solitary confinement' – under protest, either in a grand contralto or a deep bass, perhaps depending on mood. A few days later he went home on leave and sent a letter in advance pointing out to his folks that he did not want to see any 'fodder' out of tins whilst at home – 'twiggez-vous?' (15 November 1915).

Billie tended to have interesting exchanges with local civilians, especially in Dernacourt (near Albert), for instance, with an extremely elderly 'Madame' who claimed to be a 'Mam'selle'. In order to test out her resolve Captain Nevill gallantly asked her to marry him. An early bird, he once surprised the owner of the Café de la Jeunesse, Rosamunde, with her hair in paper curlers. He also offered her his hand in marriage.

Being armed, as he was, with these sorts of local encounters, Billie was one of the founders of the 18th Division magazine, one month before *The Wipers Times* was established. The historian of the division described this production as 'sprightly'. Other sources claimed that Billie Nevill wrote the whole thing himself and it was very bawdy, with a whole lot of local anecdotes, such as the one about the lady in hair curlers.

Billie Nevill was killed on the first day of the Battle of the Somme, 1 July 1916. Before the 8/East Surreys went over the top he distributed some footballs amongst his company, challenging them to kick the balls all the way to the German trenches, with a prize for the winner. On one of these balls he scribbled: 'The Great European Cup-Tie Final. East Surreys v. Bavarians. Kick-off at Zero.' On another he wrote in big letters: 'NO REFEREE!' The balls were found in captured enemy trenches the next day. Billie lasted only a few seconds after leading his company over the top.

The Wipers Times

It was possible that *The Wipers Times*, which, along with its successors, became arguably the most famous trench journal, owed something to Billie Nevill's creation. Look at the issue for 22 May 1916: 'How much money changed hands when it was known he didn't get married on leave?'

On 29 May there was a message for 'Sadie' to let her know that 'he' had not married his platoon and thus there was still a chance for her.

By 1 December 1916, *The Wipers Times* had become *The BEF Times* in order to avoid letting the Germans know where the editors were. The matrimonial column of the new production was vastly popular in trenches full of sex-starved soldiers. The journal claimed that it was receiving thousands of advertisements for this enterprise and was planning 'A Grand Christmas Number' to take account of this demand for space ('if the paper arrived in time'). All in all, *The Wipers Times* and all its progeny catered very well for the 'harassed subaltern' – for whom it cared deeply. 'Are you unhappy?' it asked them. 'Is your life miserable?' 'Do you hate your company commander?'

In order to address the last of these situations the newspaper offered its brand-new patented duckboard. If you trod on one end, the other would rear up and strike the company commander a crippling blow to the head. It came in three sizes, each one guaranteeing a Blighty One for the company commander.

The correspondence column also remained highly significant, sustaining the quality demonstrated by the acrimonious dispute over the cuckoos along the Menin Road. Indeed, this famous and notorious avenue featured very frequently – for instance, highlighting the suspected police speed trap along it.

Philosophy and innovation, too, remained rife. 'Who invented the Ypres Salient? Why?' *The Somme Times* reached a peak of ingenuity when it reported the development of the 'Parrotigeon' – a cross between a parrot and a pigeon, capable of delivering messages verbally.

Meanwhile, rises in property continued to be featured.

Lieutenant-Colonel Thorp

Lieutenant-Colonel Thorp was the commander of the 90th Royal Garrison Artillery Group (Heavy Guns), a highly efficient leader but stiff and starchy in manner. He did not suffer fools gladly and was very severe on his subordinates. Arthur Behrend became his adjutant late in 1916 and suffered like everyone else who worked

Lieutenant-Colonel
Thorp, Royal Garrison
Artillery.

for the tyrant. Yet Behrend, over the months, noticed another and far more attractive aspect of Thorp's personality – what you might call a wry whimsicality. For instance, the code words he used for prearranged shoots were rather old-fashioned girls' names, e.g. Clarice, Dolly, Gertie, Fanny, Pansy, Lilly, Nell, Lizzy and Tina. When Thorp also selected Yvonne, Behrend, not himself bereft of a certain humour, wondered whether 'she' reminded Thorp of a dim and distant weekend in Paris.

One Sunday morning, Corps Command instructed Thorp to aim at four targets in quick succession. He chose Matthew, Mark, Luke and John.

Having a CO like Thorp eventually encouraged attempts at comedy from his officers, but one had to tread carefully because it would have been very easy to overstep the mark, and you'd be for it then. Anyway, early in 1917 Thorp ordered tactical reports from his gunnery senior officers at 11 a.m. and 4.30 p.m. every day. Quite often there was nothing to report yet he insisted that there was always something, however trivial it might seem.

Well, this was encouragement to emulate Thorp's whimsies and prompted accounts like: 'The Germans were wearing grey-green uniforms and had a nice bailing-out tin with a long handle and they also had red blankets in their dugouts' and 'The Germans had a clean change of under-linen in the dugouts and they wear pink pyjamas at night'. But the officers who wrote these masterpieces baulked at actually sending them to the formidable Thorp.

Thorp was so keen on his job that he steadfastly refused to go on leave; apparently there was only a spinster sister at home anyway. Eventually, the general more or less insisted that Thorp take a break after none for two years. Whilst he was away his deputy was asked to recommend an NCO for the award of a French military medal. Behrend reminded the major that Thorp despised awards of any sort. But Major Pargiter persisted and Behrend put forward RSM Oatley's name.

Thorp was not pleased at all on his return to learn that the general had arranged a parade in which senior French staff officers would present the Médaille Militaire to Oatley. This medal was no joke: it carried a pension of 100 francs a year. For his part, Oatley had no idea how he had come to win it: he just did his job. A French general pinned the grand affair to Oatley's chest and kissed him on both cheeks and then turned to Lieutenant-Colonel Thorp and kissed him too. That little, lop-sided grin spread across that normally grim visage.

Behrend observed the same puckish smile during the German advance of March 1918, when things became hairy for the artillery as well as the infantry. Logistics fell apart. Thorp informed the brigade major that he had to have 500 gallons of petrol by the next day. The major licked his purple pencil and wrote, '500 gallons of petrol' on a scrap of paper, and Thorp also told him that his 700 gunners would run out of food by the next morning. The brigade major scribbled away desperately, and then they glanced at one another, and both instantly became aware of the utter absurdity of the situation and they smiled seraphically.

Lieutenant-Colonel Thorp's sketch for his artillery's new crest (1917). The theme was 'the Early Bird Catches the Worm'.

Armistice celebrations were in full swing for the Heavy Artillery Group. A mess orderly poured neat gin by mistake into Thorp's mug. But the senior gunners, spotting the chance for a bit of fun, instructed the orderly to leave the gin in the mug; it was enough to put anyone under the table. The colonel tossed back the 'water' and a faint look of surprise was rapidly followed by that crooked grin. He could certainly take his liquor.

At the party which followed, Thorp absolutely staggered the officers by rendering *My Old Dutch* and *Knocked 'em in the Old Kent Road* and other Albert Chevalier songs in an authentic Cockney accent. The stunted body and bowed legs added greatly to the mimicry. Colonel Thorp's war was over.

Bruce Bairnsfather

From his sketches on dugout walls and the like (by popular request of the inmates), Lieutenant (later Captain) Bruce Bairnsfather's genius spread to the magazine *The Bystander* in London. At the centre of his work was the character 'Old Bill'. Hundreds of Tommies became ready to swear that they were the original models for Old Bill (when you look at a lot of the pictures they may well have had a point).

Bruce Bairnsfather at St Yvon, Christmas 1914. Reproduced by kind permission of Tonie and Valmai Holt.

47

Bairnsfather was an efficient and brave machine gun officer. He was badly wounded in 1915 and sent back to England. Initially, the War Office disapproved of his cartoons but eventually bowed to their widespread popularity (even amongst the Germans) and appointed him as an official cartoon officer. Some of his cartoons are shown in this book.

In common with other officers in this chapter, Bairnsfather had a wry sense of humour to go with his art. On one occasion he took the chance, along with fellow officers, to have a bath. These tubs were situated in the local asylum and, as they were scrubbing furiously away, the inmates provided a captive audience. According to Bairnsfather, they would soon be in the army under the group enlistment system.

When he was billeted near Neuve-Eglise early in 1915, a farmer's wife was an expert thief of the officers' bully beef and dry biscuits. She employed a disabled labourer and paid the poor fellow exclusively in bully beef and biscuits. Bairnsfather rechristened the premises 'Fleecem' in deference to Flemish spelling.

Bruce Bairnsfather was blown up in the Second Battle of Ypres in 1915 and on arrival in London described himself as 'A Fragment from France', the title of his first book of collected cartoons.

Lieutenant Tyndale-Biscoe

Lieutenant Julian Tyndale-Biscoe was a subaltern in the Royal Horse Artillery, a high-spirited, rather misunderstood (at least, according to him) young man. He loved a joke and a jape; for instance, at a conference at Brigade HQ in 1916 to review possible obstacles which might affect raids in the Arras sector. A like-minded colleague of Tyndale-Biscoe's suggested that a possible problem might be resistance put up by the enemy. The colonel patiently asked them to take the meeting seriously, so Tyndale-Biscoe suggested bullet-proof tubes, 10 feet in diameter, with internal handrails. These could hold up to ten soldiers using the rails as a treadmill to roll the tubes over trenches.

Around about the same time there was an inter-battery football tournament followed by plenty of booze, and all Tyndale-Biscoe can recall is singing, *Why did Whaley swallow Jo-Jo?* He didn't have a clue who Whaley and Jo-Jo were but he knew the words from somewhere. They then retired to the guns and fired off a big one at ultimate range. Artillery officers had to account for every shot, using reasons like 'retaliation' or 'registration'. On this occasion they selected 'jubilation'. These young subalterns were not long out of school and sometimes they behaved like schoolboys; with possible death around the corner who can blame them?

Tyndale-Biscoe was at his battery's observation post early one morning when he realised that it was 1 April (1916), so he sent a bogus target to his adjutant. It was 'X38' but each sector only had thirty-six squares. It was only meant as a prank to make the adjutant an April Fool, but the major was half asleep and he sent the target on to Divisional HQ and they told the big guns to fire on X38. Officers and men stood around in the rain debating where it could be.

When they decided it didn't exist a different sort of flak started to fly around. Tyndale-Biscoe had to confess to his colonel and later that day a fellow subaltern told Tyndale-Biscoe that he was wanted at HQ to explain himself. But when he turned up no one was expecting him. He was the April Fool. Actually, the general thought that 'X38' was a jolly jape. Humour triumphed once again.

Tyndale-Biscoe was in front of his battery's observation post one night in April 1916, not very far from the enemy lines. He was up a tree trying to get a better view. But some branches were in the way and he proceeded to saw them off, hoping that Jerry would not see or hear him. He consoled himself with the thought that if he was shot out of the tree they could bury him where he fell because the tree was in a cemetery.

Buffalo Bill

A company commander in the 2/RWF was known as 'Buffalo Bill' on account of his frequent threats to shoot men if they didn't obey his orders or quickly enough. One of the Fusiliers who suffered in this way (he wasn't actually shot) was a believer in the transmigration of souls. He claimed that in a former life Buffalo Bill had been a slave-driver, and in a later life a great general, and that in the next one he would be a Bengal tiger.

In November 1914 Buffalo Bill had a cow in a trench near Fromelles to provide fresh milk. One day it escaped into no-man's-land, and in a furious temper he threatened to blow out the brains of the cow hand, or 'cow major', who was supposed to be keeping an eye on the animal. Like all the other men in the company, the cow major was more scared of Buffalo Bill than Jerry, so he leapt over the parapet and went off in search of the cow in full view of the enemy.

Buffalo Bill did a rapid calculation and decided that the cow was more expendable than the cow major. 'Come back, you bloody fool,' he screamed at the scampering figure.

Too late; the German artillery had spotted the cow and blown it up. Meanwhile, a sniper picked off the cow major, but it was only a Blighty One, so the story had a happy ending (but not for the cow).

In March 1915 Buffalo Bill came up with another wheeze. This was employing a big French dog to pull a cart up to the front line at Bois Grenier. He calculated that one of these dogs could convey the same amount of supplies and ammunition as six Tommies. He managed to 'acquire' such an animal (the farmer who owned it spent months trying to find it), and he appointed a 'dog major' to supervise the operation.

On its first trip, when it reached the corduroy track 'Dog' veered off to the left and tipped over the cart and all its contents. The dog major patiently put it all back again, but just then a shell exploded nearby and Dog leapt into a large shell hole and refused to budge. It took the dog major an hour to get it out – it was a very large dog.

Off they went again but every few yards Dog decided he'd had enough. The upshot was that the Fusiliers had to carry all the stuff themselves – and Dog. Dick Richards did suggest shooting it and claiming that it had been hit by enemy fire but they were pretty scared of Buffalo Bill. The Fusilier who believed in the transmigration of souls said that Dog had the souls of ten old soldiers and ten Indian crows, neither famous for co-operation and hard work.

Reports of Dog's conduct were taken back to Buffalo Bill but he was undeterred. He took the view that with the right sort of experience

Dog would come good. It was housed in a nice kennel heavily protected by sandbags. In the morning the sandbags were in tatters, having been the target of bayonet thrusts by Fusiliers passing in the dark. Buffalo Bill was livid and rushed around threatening mayhem with his revolver. However, during the day a whizz-bang blew the cart to pieces. Dog just hung around and the Fusiliers got to quite like him. He wasn't daft; he learnt how to flatten his body against the fire step when he heard the whine of a shell and not to go over the parapet for a stroll during the day.

They took him with them when they went to the rest areas and unfortunately, one day, Dog got lost in Béthune. A few months later men of another 2/RWF Company were in the town when Dog came up to them wagging his tail and followed them back to the front line. Eventually, he ended up in the transport lines, occasionally going up to the trenches. He was killed near Ypres in 1917, miles behind the front line.

Other Officers

Lieutenant John Glubb had fond memories of his brigade major – Captain Daly. In Monchy on 16 May 1917 the 5/Borderers' band was practising the tune of *The Old Rustic Bridge* all day long. Daly sent a signal to the Borderers' CO: 'Please inform the CO of 7th Field Company, RE as soon as your bridge is ready as they wish to demolish it as soon as possible.'

'What bridge?' the CO signalled back, somewhat bewildered.

'Sir, your old rustic bridge,' re-signalled Daly.

Glubb passed Daly one day in late July 1917. 'I say, Glubb, old boy, I've got a job for you,' he said, in his usual breezy fashion.

Glubb, being a very co-operative and efficient young officer, stood forward smartly to carry out orders.

'Yes,' continued Daly, 'get one or two of your fellows to put railings round my canvas bath to stop the general falling in it every morning.'

Major Eric, commander of an artillery battery at the Battle of Passchendaele, was often bad-tempered under the considerable stress of trying to support the infantry in this dreadful terrain, but he had his lighter moments. He had a habit of calling out to his gunners as he strode out to them in the morning. 'Who's winning the war?' he would shout.

The gunners were expected to reply loudly, 'They are, sir.'

Back at HQ, Eric declaimed: 'You can still see the muzzles of the guns sticking out of the water so that's all right: we can still fire them. But I wonder if they've got any big boats. We could advance with the guns if we could put them on boats.'

'Ian Hay' also had amusing tales to tell about his CO in a battalion of the Argyll and Sutherland Highlanders (1915), who professed that he liked the odd whiff of enemy gas because it wiped out the infernal flies. When it didn't materialise one day he ordered a subaltern to take a shilling over to the Jerries. When the cheeky lieutenant, playing the game, replied that he would need a mark (German currency), the CO indented for 'a surgical operation' for the young man.

A padre who was with the 2/RWF for a spell in 1915 was famous for being able to drink the battalion quartermaster under the table, a feat hitherto unknown. On his first visit to the trenches he drank every officer dry so he didn't get a drop second time round. The Fusiliers reckoned that when this man of God 'went west' he would finish up in hell in charge of the biggest bar they had.

Lieutenant Birchell (Oxon and Bucks Light Infantry), in quiet moments of reflection on the war, decided that he strongly objected to large objects of an explosive nature being thrown at him because they might hit him. The only result would be that his few remains would be collected in a sandbag and buried by ribald soldiers and thrown out a few days later by a German shell. No, Lieutenant Birchell wanted to die at 95 and be buried by the vicar at a funeral attended by the old ladies of the parish.

The CO of the 4.5 Howitzer Battery was frequently asked about the green and pink medal which he sported on his chest. 'L'ordre du Merité,' he would explain proudly. 'I got it at Bullecourt. I was digging out a gun pit when I came across the regalia of the Mayor of Arras. Look, this is a pretty important decoration, you know, old boy. But I'm not so popular with the citizens at the moment. The French Mission are saying I've been deliberately shooting at a

Cartoon by F.H. Townsend.

crucifix outside a church. Actually, I was aiming at a pigeon. I'm short of practice, you see.'

Major George Ardagh of the Royal Fusiliers was fondly known as 'Little Four-by-Two'. He had been in the army for many years before the war. In August 1914, on hearing the news of the outbreak of war, he paid for his own passage from Rhodesia so that he could join his battalion in France as soon as possible. Ardagh was very short and thin but was in the trench day and night amongst his men, chatting on the fire step and smoking his pipe. But he needed looking after, especially at night. When moving about he relied on a small group of admirers to guide him safely around and pull him out of sump holes and latrines and the like. He was like a friendly uncle.

This was an aspect of brotherhood often overlooked in views of this war. The officers in this chapter were considered highly amusing by the Tommies, and regarded with affection, apart from Buffalo Bill.

FOUR

Brass Hats

Comic Brass Hats

Generals and their staffs performed their duties generally behind the trench lines so were therefore an easy target for ridicule – not always deserved – from officers and other ranks who had to endure the front line. Generals, brigadiers and colonels were commonly known as 'Brass Hats' and their staffs of majors, captains and even lieutenants as staff officers. However, there were comedians amongst their own ranks (as shown by the example of Captain Daly in the previous chapter). Others were at least good for a laugh; Major-General Shae was frequently seen in the trenches, for example on 27 March 1916, when he was warned that there was a sniper around.

'A snip-ar!' he snapped, in his posh and fruity voice. 'A snip-ar, o, is thar the dirty blight-ar!'

So saying, he stuck his head above the parapet, screwed his monocle into place and had a good look around. He had just lowered himself when a bullet smacked into the parados behind him.

When in the trenches Shae was always checking whether men had their gas masks with them. This was a sincere concern for their safety. One day he actually forgot his own mask and had to borrow one – they were carried around in a bag. Later, he spotted a soldier without one and presented him with the borrowed bag. The private opened the bag and discovered inside only a pair of filthy old socks, put there, possibly, by another 'dirty blight-ar'.

General Plumer was affectionately known as 'Daddy' to rank and file, and 'Drip' to subalterns due to a sinus problem. In May 1915 Lieutenant Tyndale-Biscoe, whom we met a few pages ago, arrived in the Ypres Salient with the Royal Horse Artillery, where they were immediately inspected by Daddy. The lieutenant had a rather wild horse – cunning, vicious and shaped much like a hippopotamus. It had been christened 'The Kaiser'. It took one look at Daddy and aimed a formidable back leg at him. Lucky he missed, because Daddy was an important member of Field Marshal Haig's command team.

A brigade major was attached to an Australian unit. The Australians were notoriously immune from deference to officers. The major, like Major-General Shae, had a monocle and the Aussies' idea of a joke was to appear in front of him with half-crowns stuck in their eyes. The staff officer's response to this was swift and stunning: he put the eyepiece on his finger and thumb, flicked it in the air and caught it in his eye. 'There you are, do that, you clever barstards,' he snapped breezily.

Other Brass Hats and staff officers raised a smile or two simply by appearing on the scene. Lieutenant Richard Hawkins, 11/Royal Fusiliers, recalled a visit by Lieutenant-General Maxse, who was 5 feet 6 inches tall, and his aide-de-camp Captain Montague, who was 6 feet 3 inches.

The major-general of the Royal Artillery was nicknamed 'Pork Butcher'. He was inspecting a heavy gun brigade and, as usual, said 'Splendid, splendid!' a lot. He noticed the inscription 'Inspected in GIB' on the side of one of the guns. 'I had no idea these guns had been to Gibraltar,' he observed, in some surprise.

In fact, GIB stood for General Inspection Branch, which, to all intents and purposes, was run by Pork Butcher.

Lieutenant-General Sir Richard Haking (or 'Bulldog' Haking) was fond of chatting and laughing with the old soldiers who came to France and Flanders in 1914. Whilst inspecting the 2/RWF in 1915 he joked with the veterans, pinching their arms and ears, asking how many children they had and whether they could be doing with some leave to produce some more. But it could have been Haking whom Siegfried Sassoon was referring to in his poem *The General* – 'he did for them all by his plan of attack'.

Lieutenant-General Fanshawe was the 'Chocolate Soldier', or 'Fanny', who had the lovely habit of presenting chocolate to subalterns whom he thought had done well – for instance to Lieutenant Edwin Vaughan at Authieule on 27 July 1916. It just showed how young these officers were. Vaughan got his reward by being able to reel off the names, numbers, ages, civil occupations and details of the families of the men in his platoon.

Brigadier Hunter-Weston of VIII Corps was elected to Parliament in October 1917. On hearing the news he strode outside HQ and invited (bemused) Tommies to heckle him. 'Go on,' he insisted, 'ask me any questions you like. I'm a Member of Parliament now. I have been honoured by my fellow citizens.'

But they didn't have a clue what to ask him (apart from whether he had a spare fag). Perhaps they thought of something later on.

Ridicule

Beyond these examples, the overriding humorous element in connection with Brass Hats is contained in the epithet 'velvet-arsed barstards'. *The BEF Times* for 8 September 1917 had two definitions for 'duds': the first was a shell which did not explode; and the second often drew a large salary and exploded for no reason.

A Lewis gun officer of the 6/Connaught Rangers (27 January 1918) pointed out that the further you got from the battle zone the more 'offensive' officers were. This concept of 'offensive' was contained in a pamphlet sent out by an army school 30 miles behind the front line many times since 1916 and headed up 'Am I offensive enough?', a question, the pamphlet urged, every subaltern should ask himself every morning as he awoke in his dugout. Obviously it was designed to reduce complacency at the front line but it meant something different there, as implied by *The Wipers Times* of 1 May 1916.

Lieutenant Dane blamed staff officers for mixing tea and sugar in rations sent up to the trenches; for labelling jam 'Plum and Apple' when it was clearly made of something else; hiding barbed wire in hedges; and the weather. If it wasn't them, who was it then?

Not surprisingly, staff officers got short shrift at the sharp end of the front, especially from colonial troops. In March 1917, near Arras, a senior British officer popped down below to visit some New Zealand tunnellers working hard underground. 'Do you think Fritz can hear you?' he enquired.

'They'll have to be bloody f***ing deaf if they can't,' was the terse response from the ANZAC.

It was no wonder that when a couple of ANZACs caught sight of a very fat British staff officer attached to their unit one turned to the other and observed, 'Say, Alf, that's where all our rations go.'

As a greeting to another staff officer some Tommies propped up a German corpse on the fire step with a lighted candle in its hand and a fag in its mouth. The Brass Hat walked straight past it without a second glance.

Questionnaires from HQ

Staff officers, indeed, had to justify their continued membership of a general's entourage. Perhaps this was one of the reasons for the stream of bizarre demands and advice which poured out from their pens and pencils. Lieutenant Eberle was sent such a document in 1915 with no less than eleven headings. He was asked whether it was a good idea to issue flypaper to the trenches and how long it would last. Eberle also had to say how many pipe-fitters there were in his unit and how many hairdressers, chiropodists and bicycle repairers. Lieutenant Lancelot Dykes Spicer (2/4 King's Own Yorkshire Light Infantry) was quizzed by his Brigade HQ on 9 November 1915. How many men were left-handed, how many had red hair, how many had not been christened and how many had not cut their toenails during the previous fortnight and why?

Runners brought all manner of such demands daily. The following is what was received by a battalion of the Oxon and Bucks Light Infantry on a day in May 1915:

1. Hold frequent respirator and smoke helmet drills. The signal for respirator drill will be two Cs on the bugle.
2. Have you got a fully qualified Welsh miner who can speak fluent French and German?
3. Ignore message 1. The signal for respirator drill will be two blasts on a whistle.
4. A French aeroplane with slightly curved wings, giving it the appearance of a German one, is known to be in your vicinity. Use your discretion in accordance with Anti-Aircraft Regulations, para 1, section 5.
5. Report the number of windows of smoke helmets broken since you were in the trenches. The signal for respirator drill will be two blasts on a shell gong and not as message 3, which corrected message 1.
6. Re message 4, for the word 'French' read 'German' and for the word 'German' read 'French'. Still use your discretion.

The brigadier-general and his staff arrived the next day at 11.15 a.m. to ensure that everything which had been dug out during the previous night should be filled in, and everything which had been filled in should be dug out. They all left at 11.16 a.m., leaving Oxon and Bucks officers in 'a state of coma'.

A.S. Dolden recalled a divisional order to stand-to for a gas raid or 'stunt' from midnight to 1 a.m. At the same time they were also instructed to put their watches back to midnight at 1 a.m. in accordance with Daylight Saving. Dolden's company obeyed both orders to the letter and stood to from midnight to 1 a.m., put their watches back to midnight and then stood-to for another hour.

Captain Philip Berliner of the 2/7 Londons received a request from HQ to send on the false teeth of 351688 Private C.L. Blount, which had been inadvertently left behind in a trench. Berliner was under a severe enemy bombardment at Poelcappelle at the time. Guy Chapman was also suffering from enemy shelling when a note from the area sanitary officer reached him complaining about the condition of the grease-traps in Chapman's horse lines. A runner had spent five very dangerous hours bringing up this note.

Captain R.A. MacLeod of 241 Battery, Royal Field Artillery had a phone call from HQ at midnight asking how many size 6.4 boots his battalion were issued with on the previous Wednesday. At 1 a.m. another call asked for a report on what was visible from MacLeod's observation post. At 2 a.m., how many men in the battery have had no leave in the past year? At 3 a.m., how many horses in your battery have died of colic in the last year? At 4 a.m. MacLeod was asked what the average number of children was per soldier in his battery; at 6 a.m., how many miles of cable had been used in the last fortnight and what for? Captain MacLeod was of the opinion that the list of possible questions was endless. The 'winner', he suggested, was the one who guessed most of the answers.

Messages were received by the 2/RWF in trenches at Hulluch to the effect that the lieutenant-general was worried about defeatist talk and too much foul language. Dick Richards was the bearer of these tidings and his company commander swore vividly at him and continued in the same vein for the whole afternoon. The general was also concerned about buttons which were not shiny enough, but the captain reckoned that if they shone every button the battalion would resemble thousands of heliographs as they moved up to the front, giving enemy observation a splendid view of troop movements. He further theorised that the general was chief director of a metal polish company.

Preparing for Visits from Brass Hats

It was no wonder that Charles Carrington, up to his neck in urgent preparations for the Somme at Gommecourt, was not pleased at the news that a real nuisance of a brigadier was on his way to pay a rare visit to the trenches. Carrington duly arranged for a stream of stinking sewage to block up the communication trench. Second Lieutenant Eberle was just as satisfied observing another brigadier blessed with an enormous belly. As he breezed into the trench a fragment of shell went skimming overhead and he flung himself headlong into thick, stinking mud (30 May 1915), sliding along on that gigantic gut.

The 6/Connaught Rangers were carefully coached before the arrival of a general to inspect them at Rossignal on 13 April 1917. They were particularly instructed on what their precise function was in the battalion. On the day, the general stopped by a ranger who was concentrating hard on getting it right. 'Are you a Catholic?' enquired the general.

'No, sir,' replied the keen Ranger. 'I'm a rifleman.'

The Commander-in-Chief

Soon after his appointment as CIC, Sir Douglas Haig had lunch in the Rue de Bon Enfants in Armentières, the best restaurant in town. Perhaps he was unaware (or his entourage was) that upstairs was also the classiest brothel in town.

A temporary detachment of the Artists' Rifles was in Bavincourt near Arras in the spring of 1917, guarding Field Marshal Haig and his HQ. Private Alfred McLelland Burrage, a writer in civvy street, was given the job of sweeping the path outside the great man's front door. Burrage and a comrade got what muck there was into a neat pile and then Burrage sent the other man to find something to put it in. Moments later Haig fairly flew out of the door. Burrage sprang to attention and gazed into the middle distance as military discipline obliged him to.

'I don't want you to stand to attention,' snapped Haig. 'I want to see you get your work done, not standing about here doing nothing. Go on, man, sweep that dust up and then go.'

Burrage did exactly as he was told: he swept the muck to one side and then cleared off. Later on, he was interrogated by his sergeant as to whether his orders to sweep the path and put the muck in a tin had been carried out. 'Your orders were countermanded,' Burrage took pleasure in reporting.

'Countermanded? Who by?'

'The CIC,' Burrage informed him gleefully. 'Orders is orders.'

Panto

Follies

There was a fair amount of actual pantomime on the Western Front – divisional shows, follies, etc. One in Poperinghe in 1915 had some unscripted ad-lib when the Germans launched one of their periodic bombardments on the town. 'Pop' was a much-loved resting place, providing attractions such as Talbot House ('Toc H'). Jerry deliberately aimed to disturb this peace.

The town major was nervous about having hundreds of men sitting in a hall which was under fire. He sent the tenor, still with half his make-up on, rushing back on to the stage to announce an official evacuation. The audience was very reluctant to go because the next act was two 'girls' – 'Ack Emma' and 'Pip Emma' (previously real girls called 'Lanoleen' and 'Vasaleen'). There was loud jeering and only a half-hearted attempt to leave. Meanwhile, the comic appeared at the back of the hall trying to hurry everyone out and shouting, 'Anyone want to buy a dugout, going cheap!'

There was another comedian at a concert given by Lena Ashwell at Arraines-sur-Somme on 19 January 1916. It was held in the Hôtel du Commerce. This funny man thought he was going down very well because the audience was roaring with laughter. What he didn't realise was that a drunk had come out on the stage behind him and was making violent love to a large broom.

At a concert given by the 2/RWF in Beuvry, on 5 April 1916, a Scottish sergeant was reeling off a string of obscene jokes as the chaplain arrived. However, the comedian was in full flow and declined to desist. Two officers leapt on to the stage but still the Billy Connelly of the Great War refused to budge and the result was a free-for-all and, apparently, the chaplain was against violence more than sex.

Another favourite at Pop was the 'Kernel of the Nuts'. This was Basil Hallam, a singer of popular ballads well known in music halls at home. A 'Nut' (or 'K'nut') meant an over-dressed young man, such as the character in the song *Gilbert the Filbert*, one of Hallam's hits. Hallam was famous for his florid suits and shoes. He was a balloon observer and was unfortunately killed over the Somme battlefield in 1916.

J.B. Priestley had the job of employing entertainers for the 4th Army near the end of the war. It was not unusual for him to receive requests like, 'Please supply two comedians, two female impersonators and as many baritones as you can find'. Perhaps he could have used the lusty Fusilier of the 2/RWF, who at Christmas 1917 enhanced a company sing-song with a robust rendering of *La Donna é mobile* without any front teeth.

In fact, there were plenty of 'Dames' about. In March 1918 the Artists' Rifles, in headlong retreat near Albert, discovered the costumes of a hastily departed concert party, and some of the more audacious Artists quickly became Dames. Other units coming rapidly past still had time to make numerous indecent proposals.

You didn't need professional actors for some pantomime. Lieutenant-General Hunter-Weston was delivering a stirring and rallying speech to two newly arrived battalions (Warwickshire Territorial units) who were joining his 4th Division on the Somme (22 June 1916 – a few days before the great battle). Hunter-Wilson exhibited jingoism at its best: 'Leap over the parapets! Kill the Germans! Kill them all! Spike them! Stab them! Stick your bayonet into them!'

Directly in front of him sat the Irish padre, Macready, eyes bulging with patriotic fervour. Suddenly he sprang into the air twirling his shillelagh round and round his head. 'Hurrah!' he screamed in a wild Gaelic salute. 'Hurrah!' It was infectious. The Territorials sprung to their feet and cheered uproariously for Britain.

There were more vicarious entertainments available. Charles Edmonds noticed general amusement at the antics of Jerries under shellfire, scurrying about like 'blue-arsed flies'. No doubt Jerry had the same sort of fun watching the Tommies rushing to and fro under instructions from the latest guru who knew where the next shell was going to fall.

Certainly anyone with a view of the ramparts at Ypres during enemy bombardments could get some black amusement out of the shots which fell into the canal and provided free showers for dirty troops.

A little French general passed a detachment of the Artists' Rifles every day at Bavincourt in April 1917 going along to report to Field Marshal Haig. Every time they saw him Private Burrage called out: 'Party will march at atten-shun! Party – 'steen-hun!' And every time this happened the little general's horse reared up and shook him all over the place whilst he was calling desperately, 'As it was! As it was!'

Dress

Because of the atrocious conditions, officers and men alike assumed (even in 1914) a tramp-like appearance – balaclavas on their heads, sandbags around their legs, enormous overcoats, often hanging in ribbons, and the whole lot plastered in mud (see Bruce Bairnsfather's drawing of himself in 1915). They got used to it because the alternative was to be permanently frozen and soaked to the skin.

In 1915 Lieutenant R.H. Mottram reported to HQ on the state of play at his section of the front. But it was he who was in a state. He had a woolly sleeping cap on his head, his uniform was soaked and torn in half. Over this was draped a blood- and muck-smeared raincoat overlaid by a private's web equipment. Sandbags were wrapped around his shins and over boots which squelched as he moved. He was leaning on the branch of a tree which he used to test the depth of the water in the trench before wading in. His reports were thus received with a certain amount of caution.

Under-garments also suffered. Some men refused to bother with them eventually, especially as pants were popular with lice. At

Loading up Tommy.
Drawing by Bruce
Bairnsfather. Reproduced
by kind permission of
Tonie and Valmai Holt.

Erquinghem, on the outskirts of Armentières, late in December 1914, Dick Richards of the 2/RWF was persisting with them but his existing pair finally gave up. Searching around some of the grand but ruined houses of the town he found a magnificent pair of lady's bloomers. Unfortunately, soon after, Dick was due at the baths for a delousing and could not hide the new underwear from his mates, Duffy and the 'Old Soldier', and they gave him a wolf whistle and asked for a kiss.

In March 1915 at Bois Grenier the 2/RWF were allowed 'walking-out' dress, including rifles and fifty rounds of ammunition. After a drink or two it was a popular pastime to loose off a few shots at passing aircraft in case they were German. However, on one particular night they got carried away and shot out all the bottles and glasses in a cafe and then turned their weapons on carcasses hanging up in a butcher's shop across the road. The butcher was 'dancing a two-step' round the corner and screaming for the Military Police. Walking-out dress was abolished soon after.

The situation was not made any easier by all the clobber Tommy had to cart around with him at the front, and to and from it. Even officers suffered: Robert Graves' belt in 1915 conveyed a revolver, field glasses, compass, whisky flask, wire cutter, periscope, etc., etc.

Like Dick's pantaloons, the soldiers acquired many items of local civilian attire. During the retreat of August and September 1914, the 1/Cameron Highlanders replaced their Glengarry bonnets and regulation caps with native straw hats. Captain James Jack was worried that they would be mistaken for *franc-tireurs* (snipers) if captured by the Germans and might be shot. It was at this time that Jack was using small-scale tourist cycling maps to find out where they were because the retreat had taken them off the military maps.

Four years later (1 September 1918), Jack was grappling with a more civilised problem concerning dress. His subalterns were increasingly sporting cream ties, collars and shirts, and even breeches. Jack believed this made them an easy target for the enemy, especially snipers (just like the silhouette of riding breeches and boots had made them conspicuous in 1914). But Jack received a stream of complaints from wives and sweethearts etc., pointing out that light clothes were all the rage in Britain.

Lieutenant C.M. Slack of the 4/East Yorkshires remembered an American MO (more and more American doctors were being drafted in to replace the growing number of casualties amongst British ones in 1917). Captain Tablitz was a 'funny little man' in glasses and a billycock hat with two tassels. He was very jolly and kept saying, 'I guess ...'

Fritz had interesting items of attire, too. Miners of the 175 Tunnelling Company emerged from a shaft near the enemy lines at Hooge in 1915 and spotted civilian German contractors wearing top hats. One of them was seated on a latrine but all the miners could see of him was his top hat and his bum. These were irresistible targets: the first shot struck him on the backside and the second blew away his top hat. The miners beat a hasty retreat.

Early in 1917 the Germans moved back from their Somme front to take up formidable new positions on the Hindenburg or Siegfried Line to the north and east. In order to achieve a successful withdrawal they fought holding actions. At Butte de Warlencourt on 9 February the Canadians launched a night-time raid (or stunt) against these delaying Jerries. The ground was covered in snow and an officer had taken the precaution of purchasing a hundred white ladies' nightdresses in Albert as camouflage. The tough Canadians drove into battle enveloped in voluminous nighties. The 8/ and 10/Gordon Highlanders were more modestly attired – white smocks over their kilts. It was enough to put the fear of God up Fritz. No wonder plenty of prisoners were taken; they must have been mesmerised.

Later, the London Irish Rifles, not to be outdone by these colonials, marched into Béthune in German helmets with sausages stuck in the spikes.

The snag with voluminous topcoats was that they dangled in the mud and could become so heavy they dragged the men down. The 8/Leicesters in Berles-au-Bois joined a growing practice of cutting off coat tails with razors. But a new recruit, Private Collins, went too far, with the result being that the sack pockets hung down below his knees, making him look like a cockerel. Many Scots walked around with their spoons (the prime item of cutlery given the diet of soup and soup) stuck in their socks like skean dhus.

Near the time of the abandonment of the Battle of the Somme, late in 1916, officers of the King's Shropshire Light Infantry came across a poor fellow stuck in the gluey light mud of the region. They managed to get him out but at the cost of trousers, pants and boots, which remained where they were. This was one of few ways to get new clothes out of quartermasters.

The amount of baggage officers brought to the Western Front, especially in 1914 and 1915, was incredible. If they could afford it all sorts of home comforts were taken, like Captain Daly's canvas bath. This was a headache for quartermasters, who had to arrange for all this gear to be carted around. The limit was supposed to be 35 pounds (about 16 kilos). In a Scots Regiment early in 1915 a company commander described a subaltern's load as 'half a ton of assorted lumber, enough to start a military museum on its own'.

Haircuts

Getting a haircut was a perennial problem for the soldiers. There was a preference for civilian barbers, given the basic art of the army ones – as much off as possible in the shortest possible time. As the price of the military cut was commonly a couple of fags, these military shearers were not going to hang about.

Civilian exponents of the craft were thus in heavy demand, especially the lady barber in Le Cornet Boudois, a small place near Lillers (it also had an oyster bar). But the great majority of these had fled from the rest towns, especially those prone to enemy shelling. George Coppard of the 2/Queen's was thus amazed to discover a barber at Le Bizet near a reserve trench (Armentières front) – an old man living in a cellar. His methods, however, were not dissimilar to those of his army brethren. He rapidly ploughed a furrow up the back of Coppard's head. Then the shells started whizzing over and the old boy fled precipitately without a word. Coppard shouted out that the shells were falling well away from Le Bizet and it was safe to come out.

'Fini! Fini!' yelled the barber from under his bed. Coppard had to go back to the Queen's looking like a Native American – and this provided his pals with a few days of jolly banter.

The same thing happened to John Reith (5/Scottish Rifles) on 17 December 1915, also near Armentières. Like Coppard, he was surprised to find a shop open, and with two barbers. For some reason best known to the head-shearer, his method was to style one side of the head at a time. So, inevitably, he had just completed one side of Reith's hair when shells started exploding. Both barbers fled rapidly into the basement and refused adamantly to come out. At least Reith had a servant who could complete the job. Whether he matched the other side perfectly Reith did not say (he was not a man it was safe to ridicule).

At Rest

Billeting officers had to find accommodation for resting units and the arrangements were sometimes hurried, to say the least. Captain Eberle (2nd Field Company, Royal Engineers) found an ancient lady fast asleep in the bed he was directed to occupy.

Writing about shells falling, Armentières and old ladies recalls the behaviour of a RAMC corporal on 15 September 1917. It was a severe raid and two elderly dames fled from one house clad only in blankets and made a rush for the RAMC dressing station across the road. Unfortunately, as they crossed over a shell fell very near them and they skated about in all directions. The corporal, witnessing these wild scenes, found it impossible not to start laughing – it was a bit like the Keystone Cops (the Benny Hills of the First World War). As he stood shaking at the door, a shell hit a stove behind him. Another old lady sitting next to it was unharmed; she just sat there staring blankly at the orderly.

Two artillery officers relax on a sofa in a dug-out near Zillebeke, 24 September 1917. Reproduced by kind permission of the Imperial War Museum (Q6016).

As a result, he became hysterical with manic guffaws and the two ladies in the road decided they would prefer to go back home than to the RAMC, and the old girl by the stove brushed past him and joined them.

At Herzeale near Ypres in July 1917 an officer thought he was safest in the middle of a field in a tent rather than in a house next to it. Accordingly, Lieutenant Brian Lawrence herded some cows to the edge of the pasture and directed them through the tent. The next day Lawrence, hoping for a repeat prank, found the tent surrounded by barbed wire.

Moving up to the Battle of Arras from the Somme area in April 1917, it was a journey of one-night stopovers for the 7th Field Company, Royal Engineers. John Glubb recounted how marvellous his French hosts always were. Again, arrangements could be somewhat rushed, but the inconvenience was suffered by the householders rather than the soldiers. He was provided with a very nice room at the rear of the mayor's house in Guinecourt on 5 April. It was the mayor and mayoress' bedroom and they moved into a tiny room to accommodate Lieutenant Glubb. In the morning he had to cross this room to get down to the kitchen; luckily, Madame Mayor was already downstairs cooking the breakfast – but her husband was balanced precariously on the bed trying to pull up his trousers.

Indeed, officers were very frequently provided with proper beds and bedclothes. But the one Lieutenant Eberle vividly recalled was one he tried to sleep in on 16 September 1915. This was in Foncquevillers: the bed was constructed with an ancient wooden frame circling an array of equally ancient springs – huge things about a foot high and covered only with a slack mesh of chicken wire. Eberle was given a rough and dirty canvas sleeping bag to crawl into. Each time he tried to turn over in this contraption springs would erupt violently behind or in front of him, striking tender parts of his anatomy. Alternatively, he could slide off a spring into an abyss until hit by another spring – in equally sensitive spots. He fully intended to report as walking wounded in the morning.

Some officers carried primitive portable beds around with them in order to avoid this sort of experience, along with pneumatic pillows. One servant, trying to blow up one of these with a bicycle pump

(16 August 1915), found to his cost that this was not a suitable method of expansion when it blew up in his face.

Lieutenant Eberle, still in Foncquevillers (12 October 1915), was on guard duty when three casualties reported with injuries. Their stove had blown up in their midst. They had returned from an *estaminet* one cold night and decided to get the stove going. Unfortunately, they had forgotten that they had hidden their Maconochie ration tins in the stove. A merry blaze was achieved, with the result that the tins exploded and blew out the walls of the stove. They had various cuts and bruises but hopes of a Blighty One were somewhat lowered due to the fact they couldn't stop laughing.

There was another explosion at Méricourt on 3 February 1916 on an even colder night. Servants of the 1/8 Warwickshires had got a roaring fire under way in their officers' house but were fast running out of fuel. They thus decided to raid the roof of the house next door, which was unoccupied. However, after removing a fair number of rafters there was a great roar and the servants had to beat a rapid retreat as the whole house fell down around their ears. Moreover, a great bellow of dust ballooned out of the officers' fire and covered them in muck.

Four days later, Private John Jackson witnessed more pantomime issuing from a house he was passing. Just at that moment a Jack Johnson hit it and out tore an officer of the Gordon Highlanders in his pyjamas, followed closely by his cook holding a frying pan with his officer's breakfast still sizzling in it.

A company of the 2/RWF had a nice billet in March 1915. It was a large house surrounded by a moat. New neighbours moved in, however: this was an artillery battery complete with a huge gun mounted on caterpillar tracks. It was getting ready to fire so the Fusiliers opened all their windows, stuffed paper in their ears and hid under anything available. The monster fired, reared up at a crazy angle and slid slowly into the moat, accompanied by wild applause from the house.

Corporal Ernest Parker of the DLI was strolling along one night in Arras, in September 1916, when he saw an MO in a lighted room across the way trying to remove an obviously stubborn tooth from a victim's mouth. The medic was complaining loudly about the obstinate molar and calling for assistance. Two burly orderlies appeared from within and promptly sat on the patient's shoulders. The 'dentist' then triumphantly wrenched out the offending tooth, accompanied by screams from his writhing patient. Parker continued on his way, possibly hoping that his own teeth stayed in prime condition.

As we saw in the case of Brian Lawrence, practical jokes were very common. A company commander in the Welsh Regiment (at Vermelles in June 1915) had suffered badly in the trenches and his nerves were shot to pieces. An officer 'friend' rolled an un-detonated bomb down the stairs into a cellar where the poor bloke was trying to restore his shattered morale. He just stared morosely at the bomb; he probably thought that life could not get any worse, anyway. The 'joke' was as much of a dud as the bomb. He was calculating that in a year's time the front would move less than a mile – in which direction he wasn't prepared to guess. Whether he would be there to see it he very much doubted.

We have seen how often rest areas came under fire. At Winnezeele, in January 1917, two Scots were caught out returning from a binge. One remembered that there was a shallow trench nearby and suggested to his chum that they ought to make a run for it.

'I'll be f***ed if I can,' gasped the other.

'You'll be f***ed if you don't!' warned his friend.

Tommies often tried to recreate bits of their civilian existence behind the lines. A temporary detachment of the Artists' Rifles was helping to guard Field Marshal Haig at Bavincourt in the spring of 1917. This included two former scouts: one, a scoutmaster, and the other a boy scout. They erected a tent in an orchard and covered it with the appropriate flags and badges. Sat outside this, the ex-master tested the ex-scout on scout procedures and practice. A few miles away the big guns at the Battle of Arras roared away.

Writing about boy scouts is a reminder that Lieutenant-General Congreve (affectionately known as 'General Concrete' by all who served under him) brought his 12-year-old son, Christopher John, into a trench at Hooge (22 August 1915). The boy was on holiday in France and turned up there attired in full boy scouts outfit, excited by the occasional crump of a shell (or scared out of his wits). He came round a traverse and was spotted by a sentry. 'Blimey, Bill!' exclaimed the sentry, ''ere's a bleedin' boy scaht or am I going bonkers?'

Soldiers billeted near Authie in April 1916 were provided with unscheduled entertainment when Lieutenant Eberle of the Royal Engineers was demonstrating a 'Bungalore Torpedo' (used for blowing holes in enemy wire entanglements) for senior staff officers in a field. The torpedo, however, only worked off a ten-second fuse, which meant that Eberle had that amount of time to dash across a long, open field, also including the odd shell hole or two. His frantic rush across the uneven turf was gleefully witnessed by soldiers ringing the field, and they gave him a good and rousing reception as he hurtled along in front of them.

At Parties

Officers' rags were popular amongst those who had graduated from the public schools. Lieutenant Greenwell (1/4 Oxon and Bucks Light Infantry) attended a 'tremendous' one on Boxing Day 1915. As he arrived he was handed a tumbler full of 'crème de menthe'. It was really green cracker paper soaked in water. Greenwell quickly twigged what it was and played along. He pretended to knock it back, then seized his stomach in mock alarm and rolled about on the floor in apparent agony. Then he burst out laughing and the startled guests all joined in. It was a good start to a rousing party.

Officers of 377 Battery of the 169 Artillery Brigade celebrated the birthday of their captain, Gardner, in the late summer of 1917, along the Rue Flourie in Armentières. Their CO, well-fuelled, pounded up and down the lane on his big white horse, scattering passing infantry in all directions. He reached the end of the lane and turned. 'Look out! Look out! Here comes the bugger again!' warned an amused Tommy. The evening was a huge success and the CO afterwards became widely known as 'The Galloping Major'.

On 4 January 1917 an Old Etonian dinner was staged in a grand house in St Omer. A band was playing and the chandeliers were festooned in light blue ribbons. Champagne flowed freely and the din was ear-shattering as Old Etonians screamed at one another and started throwing things. After *God save the King* had quietened them down a bit, the clamour returned and they began singing the old school songs, including *Jolly Boating Weather*. This created a crescendo of excitement and they began climbing on top of the tables, forming a traditional 'ram'. As this swayed from side to side tables started collapsing accompanied by deafening cheers.

Then the ribbons hanging from the chandeliers were seized and swung back and forth to the rhythm of the boating song. Wider and wider went the swings until the chandeliers gave way and crashed to the floor as Old Etonians scrambled to get out of the way. In the finale everything in the hall was smashed to pieces – tables, chairs, bottles, glasses and windows.

The 1/8 Warwickshires had a party in Péronne where the 'disgusting' padre challenged six subalterns to a boxing contest. After he landed several strategic hits they managed to drag him down and pull off his trousers. Lieutenants Coleridge and Scales, however, fell out and had another fight, but they finished up kissing each other and professing (innocent) undying love for one another.

Lieutenant Mottram had an interesting job in Flanders, travelling around settling civilian claims for theft, damage and debt from soldiers. He was assisted by a Belgian liaison officer whom he called 'De V.' Mottram grew very fond of De V. and was sad when he had to move south with his division. A leaving do was arranged and another Belgian officer, 'De G.', told Mottram that it was a custom for their officers bidding farewell to have knives thrown at them. Accordingly, De V. leant against a door frame, inviting his comrades to throw knives into the door. It was a quaint and somewhat risky way to say cheerio but it all went off well and all the knives missed (surprising, considering the amount of Flemish beer that had gone down their throats), and the evening was rounded off by carrying the paralytic De V. back to his billet. It was rumoured that he was descended from Charlemagne.

Baths

Delousing at baths could be eventful. George Coppard (2/Queen's) was at the pit-head baths at Sailly-Labourse, enjoying a plunge into the enormous vats. The only drawback was that there was coal dust

THE BATHS. VERMELLES.
Nov. 1916.

Drawing by I.L. Read.

everywhere, including the benches they had to sit on whilst drying. When they stood up, everyone's bum was covered in the black stuff. They wanted to rename themselves the 'Black Arse Brigade'.

The RAMC orderly at the baths in Nieppe (22 May 1915) was pure panto. He wore a fancy apron and a red jelly-bean cap with a tassel. He fussed around his customers as they climbed in and out of the vats. 'Out you get! Out you get!' he lisped at them, clearly enjoying working with all these fine fellows in their birthday suits. If they weren't quick enough he doused them in stone-cold water from a hosepipe. They all took it in good part, laughing and joking with the funny little man.

Sport

Football was the favourite game, played everywhere and at every opportunity. In the Arras sector in April 1917, a very busy time in the trenches, the 9/Royal Scots were easily the best team. Yet it was in their inter-platoon 'friendlies' that the fiercest rivalry existed. It was amazing that each platoon (less than twenty men) could raise a more-than-decent team. The deadliest matches of all were those between 2 Platoon and 4 Platoon. Sergeant Bill Hay of 4 always managed to pick a fight with a 'stroppy' sergeant of 2 Platoon by calling him 'Bollocks'.

American troops try to explain the mysteries of baseball to some Tommies (1918). Reproduced by kind permission of the Imperial War Museum (Q8847).

The Christmas truces of 1914 included football matches between the Tommies and the Jerries, although no one is too sure of the scores. A letter from Johannes Niemann recorded that he participated in hare hunting with a group of soldiers from both sides between Le Gheer and Le Touquet. This was followed by a football match which Fritz won 3-2 (no surprise there!). This game provided an opportunity for the Germans to discover what Scots wore under their kilts.

Inter-battery games for the Royal Horse Artillery near Arras in 1916 were played on a pitch containing two large crump holes. Every time the ball went down one of them two or more players disappeared after, it attempting to kick it out. The smooth, inter-passing game suffered.

Cricket was popular, usually amongst officers. Robert Graves, in Vermelles on 24 June 1915, played a game just a few hundred yards from the front line. The only bat was hewed from roof rafters and the ball was a rag tied up with string. The wicket was a parrot cage still containing the grisly remains of the parrot, which had died of starvation.

Lieutenant Eberle played even closer to the trenches at Ploegsteert – about 300 yards away. He found it difficult to concentrate fully at the wicket – one eye on the bowler and the other checking the direction of the next shell. But he managed to scrape together ten runs and his side won by 107 runs to 62.

Private George Weeks (the author's father) had one game of cricket – in Contay, where he was cutting down trees with 24/Queen's. The battalion sports officer, Lieutenant Dodridge, was keen to start up a cricket team. George wrote in his diary:

> A request was made by the Sports Officer for anyone interested in cricket and desirous to play to forward their name. Very few responses came so he came rooting around for volunteers. I was approached and after remarking that I had never played the game he answered, 'Good, everyone has to begin', and my name went into the hat as a volunteer for practice. A wicket was subsequently prepared and a scratch game

arranged. Of course, the equipment was not of the first-rate order, especially the leg guards. My turn came to wield the bat and I had begun to enjoy the game and exercise. Facing up to the Sports Officer, who had just taken the ball to bowl for the opposite team, his first delivery struck me an almighty blow on the left thigh and then four more in succession, the sixth missed me and flattened the wicket and I was helped from the scene. Back at the billet, where I was still rubbing my bruised thigh, I remarked to all and sundry how such a slightly built man could hurl a ball at such speed. A couple of the men remarked to me, 'You don't know him?' I replied, 'Of course I do – he's our Lieutenant.'

'But you don't know that he's an amateur pace bowler for Essex at home, do you?'

This information ended all my future aspirations for the future [sic] regarding my cricket. Later that evening I received a visit from Lieutenant Dodridge. He was concerned that I was practically lame and said that he had only bowled around half pace.

Inwardly, I said to myself, 'You won't ever get an opportunity to bowl at me again, not even underarm.'

His last remark before leaving was, 'You'll have to move around a bit otherwise the leg will go rigid. I'll send you a walking stick – that should help.'

I said something about what he could do with his walking stick but it escaped his hearing.

In the thick of the Battle of Loos (26 September 1915), the 2/ Lincolns attacked flanked by forty 'bombers' on each side armed with so-called 'cricket ball grenades'. Instructions for them were: 'Take bomb, tear sticking plaster off fuse, strike match, light fuse, hold for three or four seconds, throw.' But it was pelting down with rain and the Lincoln bombers reckoned that throwing real cricket balls at Jerry would do more damage (especially if thrown by the likes of Lieutenant Dodridge).

Ice hockey was sometimes played on frozen ponds and lakes. The 1/8 Warwickshires played the 7/Warwickshires at Méricourt on 25 January 1916. It was a savage contest – no quarter given. Walking sticks were used. Lieutenant Ekins came an awful cropper on the back of his head and was carted off to the hospital. The giant Irish doctor of the 1/8s wielded an enormous blackthorn and caused havoc in the opposition ranks. It was an honourable draw – no one else finished up in hospital and they all retired to the *estaminet* the best of friends.

Horse shows were popular. The 7th Field Company, Royal Engineers, held one at Souastre in June 1917. The most enjoyable race was the 'Souastre Scurry', a gallop of a quarter of a mile around a field. The riders rode bareback on lumbering dray horses – a 'blood-curdling' and 'wildly exciting' contest. Betting on the outcome was the heaviest of the afternoon. Wrestling on horseback was nearly as popular.

Sports Day for the 56th Division in the same month saw a race between chaplains and doctors on French bone-shaker bikes over very rough ground. Philip Gibbs, the famous war correspondent, reported in the *Daily Telegraph* of 4 June that the race was won by a 'long-legged C of E Padre'. This was the Rev. Julian Bickersteth.

A divisional Sports Day involving the 37 Machine Gun Company in the summer of 1917 featured real civvy street bookmakers, with cigars in their mouths, grey bowlers and money bags. George Coppard of the 37s had proved a winner in previous sack races, and since the bookies offered 10:1 on the field, a lot of money was placed on him to win. He won and the touts had one of their few bad days.

All sorts of impromptu games were held, especially by officers. Those of the 4/East Yorkshires on 14 October 1916 started a water, battle, resulting in Lieutenant C.M. Slack receiving a bucketful of very dirty stuff smack in his face.

There was a 'naval battle' on the Yser Canal near Ypres between teams of the 2/Royal Fusiliers. Rectangular boxes were the 'battleships', and they were projected along the slimy and rubbish-strewn waterway with spades for oars and nails for rowlocks. An enthusiastic crowd of supporters gathered along what was once a towpath to cheer on their favourites. Hostilities commenced with an attempt to upset an enemy craft, but the only result was that the offensive vessel whizzed round in crazy circles whilst a relieved foe made a hasty escape because their ship was only half the size of their opponent's. There were loud boos from the bank and shouts of: 'You f***ing shisters!'

Returning once more to George Weeks' diary, he described the very curious sport of hopping on one foot whilst attempting to knock your opponent over. According to George, he was very good at this game – better than at cricket, anyway. He often recounted the tale of how he defeated Private 'Chopper' Newnes in a grand final at the Royal Flying Corps No 2 Depot at Candas, north-west of Arras, in 1917. George was there patching up damaged planes. It was an epic battle until, triumphantly, George accounted for 'Chopper' with a vital lunge, depositing him in a convenient cess pit. Chopper came looking for George when he got out.

Moving Around

The speed of French trains was notoriously slow, understandably, when you consider the vast numbers of personnel and huge amount of stuff which had to be transported to the fronts. The official limit was 15 mph but 5 mph was more normal. The old BEF 'sweats' of 1914, who liked a brew-up at every opportunity, developed the habit of lighting small fires in the horse wagons for this purpose. But this was banned before the end of the year on account of the growing number of flaming trains. The Tommies couldn't understand what all the fuss was about: at the pace they were going they could throw out all their possessions and follow them on to the track.

The 2/Grenadier Guards were one of the earliest battalions to reach France in August 1914. In fact, an advanced detachment reached Rouen on the 15th. The mayor and mayoress came on board to present huge bouquets to rather embarrassed subalterns. When a second wave of the Guards arrived in Amiens on the 19th they were greeted with a caricature of the kaiser on the station yard wall. It had the face of a pig, an enormous spiked helmet and an equally exaggerated Iron Cross.

Two hundred and twenty recruits for A Company, 2/Queen Victoria Rifles, reaching Bailleul station on 30 January 1915, were heralded by the company 'band' performing on empty biscuit tins with combs: they were so pleased to get the reinforcements.

On another note, 377 Battery, Royal Artillery, beating a hasty retreat from the marauding Germans in April 1918, were greeted by a naked woman framed in an upstairs window as they tumbled into Bergicourt. Comments were not recorded.

The RSM of the 1/Cameron Highlanders was about to take up residence in a hut near High Wood (Somme) on 1 December 1916. He was only a few yards from it when it was struck by a Jack Johnson which hoisted his intended bed up on to the telephone wires. He consoled himself with the thought that in a few minutes he would have been kipping in it.

The Queen Victoria's Rifles undergoing fitness training on Hampstead Heath. Reproduced by kind permission of the Imperial War Museum and the Press Association (Q53596).

Dick Richards of the 2/RWF once travelled in style to Lieutenant-General Munro's HQ in Béthune to be decorated with the Distinguished Conduct Medal (DCM). Unfortunately, he had come straight from the trench and was covered in mud from head to foot. The general wasn't in the car but his flag was on it so the guard came out as the general's chauffeur opened the doors. They stood smartly to attention and saluted, and Dick slithered out. Happily, the guard sergeant had a sense of humour.

Another individual journey took Sapper E. Davidson to convalescence after he was wounded on the Somme. His destination was St Valery. The next morning they were awakened early and marched down to the beach accompanied by a smart band. Davidson wondered what the musicians were for; he soon found out. They started playing country dancing tunes and the invalids were lined up for a spot of square dancing. It was intended to take their minds off the war.

It certainly succeeded. Davidson found himself opposite a burly ex-bricklayer ready to dance the *Sir Roger de Coverley*. The sergeant called out the moves: 'Bow to your partner. Hold hands, advance three paces. Bow. Return three paces ...'

More Panto in the Trenches

The 7/East Kents were trying to hold the front in March 1918 against the German onslaught. A shell hit the parapet in front of Private Doug Roberts' face. Miraculously, he was unhurt, but his first instinct was to see if his 'trench family' was unscathed. To his horror, young Sidney was prostrate on the boards, his head a revolting red gunge. On closer inspection, however, Doug realised that the 'gunge' was jam, probably plum and apple. Sidney had been spooning it out when the whizz-bang had landed.

Something similar happened to Private Bishop on 16 August 1916 near Bridge 2A on the Yser Canal, just north of Ypres. Lieutenant Edwin Vaughan was just behind him and was alarmed to see a thick, red stream running down Bishop's back. 'Are you hurt, Bishop?' called the officer.

Officers of the Royal Flying Corps Kite and Balloon Section, at Bapaume, rehearse *Cinderella*. Reproduced by kind permission of the Imperial War Museum (Q8377).

'No, sir. I could do with me dinner, though.'

'But your back.'

Bishop glanced over his shoulder. 'Sod it!' he exclaimed. 'That was bleedin' strawberry, that was, sir, in me 'aversack!'

Lieutenant Lawrence Gameson noticed a Scots infantryman pulling a sodden sock over his clenched fist. This was the Somme in the extremely wet month of September 1916. Thick mud oozed out of the sock. The lieutenant was curious, to say the least. 'Can I ask what you are doing?' he enquired politely.

'Doing a spot of washing, sir,' replied the Scot cheerfully.

A new draft for the Welsh Regiment took up residence in trenches near Auchy in May 1915. One young soldier from Cardiff was desperate to get into the action as soon as possible because his brother had been killed in the Second Battle of Ypres. The men were encouraged to fire the occasional round to keep Fritz on his toes. But this bloke wanted more. He blazed away at the enemy and got

More rehearsals for *Cinderella*. Reproduced by kind permission of the Imperial War Museum (Q8378).

through two whole bandoliers of ammunition and then another handful from the bullet box. Corporal Parry should have tried to stop him but he was helpless with laughter. 'He's a f***ing Human Maxim!' he reckoned.

Sentries of the Grenadier Guards had a different reason for blazing away on the last day of 1914. Jerry had been singing carols for a whole week and the Guards were sick of them. It did the trick: 'Silent night, holy night ...' faded away. The truce was over.

Trenches were not solely constructed across open fields. They were to be found also in woods (or ex-woods), bang in the middle of villages or farms, even factories and mines. A company of the Royal Engineers were in grottoes under the cemetery in Foncquevillers during Christmas 1915. On 23 December a German mine landed amongst the graves, creating a large crater.

Following heavy rain on Christmas Day, the crater fell into the grotto which housed the sappers' kitchen, taking down 50 tons of earth and chalk and assorted civilian corpses. Finding a recently deceased lady with long, flaxen hair, and a handful of skulls amongst the pots and pans, was not welcomed by the cooks, who were halfway through cooking a Christmas feast. But, stout lads, they carried the whole lot through to another grotto and still came up on time with turkey, tinsel and Christmas pud.

The 225 Tunnelling Company were also underground on 15 May 1915. Captain Matthew Roach set a *camouflet* (a small mine) to blow up an enemy tunnel. Sadly, he cut the fuse too short, giving him and his group inadequate time to get away. The six all arrived at the foot of the escape ladder at the same time, resulting in a writhing mass of bodies on the rungs. Roach, bravely remaining at the foot of the ladder, raised a smile at a scene resembling something out of the Keystone Cops. Happily, they all managed somehow to get up the ladder before the mine went off.

Private Joe Allen was pretty low down as well, mainly on account of being 5 feet 2 inches tall. He belonged to the 109 Field Ambulance who were trying to cross a deep, water-filled shell hole to reach casualties on the Somme during the hectic days of June 1916. All his mates could see of Joe was his tin hat bobbing along the surface of the water. But he kept in step.

'You all right down there, Joe?' called Sharpy, and bubbles indicated that Joe was at least still breathing.

An unusual and rather unwanted cause of difficulty on the front line was prisoners. Command was always hoping to get some in order to get information out of them, but to Tommy they were often a bloody nuisance. First of all, where were you going to put the prisoner or prisoners if it wasn't possible right away to take them back along the communication trench?

In March 1917 Sergeant Charles had such a problem: a whole group of prisoners had to be accommodated until the following morning. He managed it somehow and he took them back to HQ. However, one of the prisoners, who was a major, complained about the treatment meted out to him during his confinement near the trenches. In fact, Charles hadn't realised that he was a major.

'He didn't say he was,' he protested to a British major. 'How was I to know he was a major unless he let on?'

Apparently, the trouble was that he had put the German major in a cellar in a house which the Germans had recently occupied, and the troops had used this cellar as a toilet. Naturally, they continued to use it as such even though their major was occupying it. They probably got a bit of a thrill doing it.

Private Smith of the 6/Connaught Rangers also had trouble with a prisoner, or, at least, a potential one. He was squatting on a latrine (Croisilles–Ecourt railway crossing, 25 November 1917) when he spotted a Jerry standing on the parapet calling 'Kamerad! Kamerad!' It was their way of surrendering. But Smithy was not ready for him. ''Ere,' he instructed, ''ands up and wait till I've finished.' Wisely, appreciating that Fritz's English might be limited, he embellished his orders with hand signals, pointing to his bum and the trousers hanging round his ankles. But Jerry was in too much of a hurry: if he stood there long enough someone might shoot him, so he cleared off further down the trench to look for a more suitable captor.

Lieutenant Lancaster of 72 Brigade, Royal Artillery, was 6 feet 2 inches tall, strikingly handsome, and popularly known as 'Husky Jake'. He had farmed for years in South America, so was regarded as a pretty tough fellow. The long nocturnal bombardments on the Somme in June 1916 were nerve-racking even for the stoutest of hearts. You crouched on the fire step under these hails of potential death wondering whether the next one would fall on you. There were so many of them it seemed hardly likely that all of them would miss.

'My God!' cried Husky Joe, quite suddenly. 'I can't stand this any longer.' He seized his gumboots, leapt over the parapet and dashed off into the night, skidding in and out of wet crump holes. He returned half an hour later completely soaked with very wet mud. He still carried the gumboots in his hand. He had taken Lieutenant Macdonald's boots by mistake. Macdonald was only 5 feet 4 inches tall.

There were actually sleep-walking Tommies. Alfred Burrage of the Artists' Rifles was one. One night in the summer of 1917 he walked 2.5 miles along the Gavrelle trenches, reaching the next-but-one battalion. His return journey, now wide awake, was fraught. Sentries who had challenged him on his way out told him in no uncertain terms how lucky he was they hadn't shot or bayoneted him.

Strangely enough, a sergeant in the same battalion of the Artists also suffered from this condition. However, he didn't go in for long, dangerous treks along trenches, but instead indulged an obviously deep, innate desire for tidiness. When he dropped off he went around making neat piles of equipment and supplies. One night he collected all his platoon's backpacks and stacked them up. He could also swear when asleep because one of the packs fell on his nose and he said, 'Bugger it!'

On the Somme front on 21 February 1917, a cook in the 2/RWF started a fire at dusk and noticed a handy piece of wood for additional fuel. In fact, this was a French SOS rocket. He was badly scorched but laughed all the way back to Blighty.

On Christmas Eve 1917 all the cooks in George Weeks' company got Blighties – not a good time for those awaiting Christmas dinner. A shell fell on their tent. The next day George was presented with a feast of currants and sultanas.

Officers made their contributions to trench fun. Denis Wheatley, the writer, habitually sported a monocle, but every time he ducked as a whizz-bang came over it fell out, to general hilarity amongst the troops. When he moved to another battalion he decided to keep his head erect at all times and earned himself a reputation for being a very brave officer.

Lastly, spare a thought for the Heavy Section, Machine Gun Corps – tanks, to you and me. These men went through agonies in these metal boxes, even if they weren't hit. Just getting into them was a trial: the 'door' measured 2 feet by 4 and they had to somehow squeeze through it. Inside, the noise and heat were terrible, not to mention the bits of metal flying about when bullets struck the tank. Because it was so noisy it was impossible to give verbal messages. For instance, when the driver wanted bottom gear, he clanged the engine casing with a hammer or a spanner – once. When he wanted second gear he banged it twice, and three times for neutral.

SIX

Pratfalls

Tumbles in the Trenches

You only have to think of the perils of slippery and unreliable duckboards, flinging yourself out of the way of flying metal in narrow, zigzagging trenches with inner walls (traverses) and the number of people moving about carrying heavy loads of equipment and supplies to realise the possibilities of slapstick in the trenches. Smart officer that he was, James Jack fell into a cesspit up to his armpits on 19 January 1915, and for once was at a loss for words.

But he was probably in a better position to get cleaned up than Dick Richards and Harry Bolton of the 2/RWF in the following month. They were actually on the surface when moving up to the Bois Grenier front, but then a sudden spell of shelling forced them to jump back into the communication trench rather hurriedly – straight into the latrines of another company. They were carrying sacks of bread, which they managed to hold aloft, even whilst sinking into the stinking mire. So the bread was saved but they weren't going to get new uniforms. Falling into latrines was not one of the qualifications for this. Consequently, when they got back to their company, old friends shunned them; no one wanted to work with them. Only the passage of time restored their popularity.

Even Bruce Bairnsfather, struggling across a dark and sodden field in November 1914, fell into a 'Johnson 'ole' at Ploegsteert.

Unfortunately, he did not later draw a cartoon of the incident (or it has been 'lost').

Alfred Burrage remembered a hectic episode around an ammunition dump at Cambrai in December 1917. A small NCO from the Hawke Battalion was trying to lead a ration party. He was struggling along himself with two petrol cans of water and two sandbags containing provisions. Even then he kept falling over, accompanied by foul obscenities. Worse was to come. The swaying sailors were met head on by a party of Royal Engineers driving along mules carrying large bundles of barbed wire. The little Hawke collided violently with a mule and went cascading into a pit.

For a few moments he lay there utterly stunned, before giving vent to a heart-rending *cri de coeur*. 'If,' he cried out in anguish, 'I ever catch that bleedin' nipper of mine playing soldiers I won't 'arf kick the little barstard's backside for 'im!'

A padre visiting the trench at Coulomby with a brigadier had a certain opinion about flinging oneself about in trenches to avoid shells. 'I am so resigned to the thought of death,' he declaimed to the staff officer, 'that I can ignore shells.' Just then, one landed on the parapet in front of them and the Brass Hat was alarmed when his companion disappeared. He eventually spotted the padre grovelling along under a couple of duckboards. He had taken an almighty dive. 'I slipped,' he explained to the brigadier.

Yet those habitually in a trench could get over-excited, even those of mature years. Private Robert Parkin of the 2/West Yorkshires was 42, toothless and from Rotherham. One day in May 1916 Parkin was knocked clean off the parapet and was convinced that his number was up. 'I'm 'it, I'm 'it!' he cried in despair, as he slid off the fire step to the boards.

'Nay, Bob,' consoled a pal, 'you're not 'it.'

'I'm 'it! I'm 'it!' insisted Parkin, and did a bit of loud groaning.

'Nay, Bob, you're not 'it at all.'

'I'm 'it!' persisted Bob. 'I tell thee, a bloody great soss an 'all on top o' t' head.'

All was soon resolved. A shell had blown out a large clod of earth and this had struck Parkin on his helmet and sent him crashing off the fire step.

As noted before, there were 'experts' on where the next shell would go, probably as many as one in every platoon (other 'experts' on 'where did that one go?' were also in demand). The soothsayers frowned mightily on the practice of throwing oneself down willy-nilly in no particular direction. Bert, as described by Anthony French, advocated closing one eye and sighting up 'the flying pig' or whatever with the other. You then raised a forefinger between eye and shell. Depending on whether the shell was to the left or to the right of your finger, you ran like hell the other way: no diving required. Mind you, there was a general acceptance of the philosophy that one of these shells 'had your name on it', placing a limit on local 'expertise'.

Somersault

Lieutenant-Colonel Feilding of the Coldstream Guards competed at the Royal Munster Regiment's Sports Day on 2 July 1917. His mare ran straight into a sandbagged wall and Feilding performed a parabolic somersault over the top of it. He crawled away with badly torn back muscles and a broken hand, to the sound of raucous applause from the men of his battalion. They liked him. He was taken to St Omer Hospital.

'Plugstreet' Wood witnessed the outcome of officers' greed for the best collection of souvenirs on the Western Front (11 June 1917). Something very interesting was seen behind the mess and an unseemly race between eager subalterns ensued. One of them opened up a considerable lead and then fell down a 5.9-pounder crump hole. All that could be seen of him were his gumboots flailing wildly in the air, and all that could be heard was a stream of foul and abusive language.

Some billets were just made for pratfalls, especially those of the agricultural kind. A company of the Black Watch were spread over five barn lofts. Barn lofts could be extremely comfortable if lots of dry straw was available. The only trouble with this one was that there was only one ladder serving all five lofts. The result was a scrum as these formidable infantrymen scrambled to get out to the *estaminets* first. The floor around the ladder finally collapsed, depositing the Black Watch on cattle minding their own business below. Neither the cows nor the soldiers seemed to mind; a few moos of protest and a few laughs, a quick dust-down and they were on their way for the 'plonk'.

Many a French or Flemish farm was commandeered for military purposes (the farmers were given compensation), and not only billeting. A Royal Garrison artillery battery, just before the opening of the Battle of the Somme, dug some big holes in a farm field and lowered their big guns into them, covering them with wire netting and earth. Unwittingly, the farmer and one of his cows strode across the field and fell in one of these holes. Because he could (roughly) follow instructions, he was extricated but the cow was a different proposition. It didn't help the gunners that they were helpless with mirth. Even a passing general had a good laugh. Given the tension attending preparations for a massive bombardment, it provided much-needed relief.

Sudden instructions to move camp behind the lines inevitably brought mayhem. If it was a transfer even further back for a long rest the excitement only made matters worse. Orders to go had a tendency to arrive at short notice. The 2/West Yorkshires received the news about two o'clock in the morning at Citadel Camp and they had to be ready to go by 6 a.m.

It was pitch dark and damp. There was wild confusion and loud imprecations as rifles fell on stockinged feet, men tripped over tent ropes and fell heavily into half-frozen mud. Someone wobbling along with a pile of blankets collided with someone with a pile of wood. Words were exchanged. But they were all blissfully happy. They were heading west and the terrible battle they had just left was to the east.

Even royalty could not escape the pratfall. The 12/Sherwood Foresters were inspected by the king after a sturdy performance at the Battle of Loos (September 1915). The Foresters put their caps on the end of their bayonets and cheered lustily – 'Hip, hip, hooray!' King George's mount reared up at this wall of sound and the monarch slid off backwards on to the pavement. A second 'Hip, hip, hooray!' lamely fizzled out, followed by an embarrassed silence. The king survived.

SEVEN

Sitcom

Communication

We met Private Robert Parkin of the 2/West Yorkshires in the previous chapter. You may recall he was 42 years of age, had no teeth and came from Rotherham. He had joined up one night when he was drunk – in Rotherham. His wife was livid the next morning but it is nice to reveal that Private Parkin survived the war and returned home to the welcome arms of the same faithful wife.

A captain noticed some captured German night flares at the back of the trench. He was short of white flares to deliver a coded message to the artillery. 'Are they white?' he asked Parkin.

'Yes, sir,' replied Parkin emphatically.

'How do you know?' demanded the captain, who had some knowledge of Parkin's limitations.

'I let one off in the latrine this morning, sir,' explained Parkin. 'It was white, sir.'

The captain suppressed a natural desire to ascertain why Parkin had let off a flare in the latrines but, being short of time, decided to accept this research evidence at face value. He gave the order to fire them. The result was a bit of a mixed bag – claret and golden rain. It was obviously a coded German message of some sort – but what? Events during the next twenty-four hours gave him the answer: claret and golden rain meant 'lengthen range'. German shells rained down on the deserted area between the British front line and the support line.

Arthur Behrend, an adjutant in the Royal Artillery, was caught up in the chaos of the retreat from the enemy onslaught of March 1918. He was racing about on his Triumph motorbike trying to locate urgently needed ammunition and supplies. But in the middle of Achiet-le-Grand the machine gave up the ghost. He slung it into a ditch in disgust. Then – he couldn't believe his good fortune – he noticed six gleaming Triumphs in a shed.

He was fiddling about trying to get one going when a corporal in the Royal Signals strolled up. 'Corporal,' Behrend called out, 'please help me to start my bike. She's a bit cold.' The corporal briskly squirted petrol into the cylinder and jumped on the kick-starter; the engine roared into life. 'Thanks awfully,' said Behrend gratefully, jumping on the machine. He whizzed off down the road.

'You're welcome, sir,' the corporal called after him; then realisation dawned. 'Hey, you, that's my bike!' He was too late.

In the confusion surrounding the Battle of Loos in September 1915, commanders could not always be sure of the identity of the unit next to them in the trenches. In these circumstances, the only way to communicate was by sending a whispered message from man to man along the trench. Lieutenants Trevor and Esson of the Royal Fusiliers received such a request from their left as they reached their new position: 'Who are you?'

Eventually, through a hundred or more whispers, the reply from Trevor and Esson reached its destination – 'Royal Fusiliers'. Ten minutes later, a further request arrived for information: 'Who's in command?'

A further ten minutes elapsed and Trevor and Essen sent their response on its way: 'Lieutenants Trevor and Esson.' And so this missive passed yet again through a hundred or more ears and mouths, and the man next to the major asking for all this vital information received the message: 'Lieutenants Trifle and Esso, sir.'

Artists

In the massive German advance of 1918 there were many anxieties, but those affecting artists in various divisional follies and shows were special. Because of the chaos they found themselves fleeing with front-line troops. The particular worry of the 'dames' was that they would be captured and their knapsacks confiscated, complete with female wigs, make-up and certain other items. They feared that Jerry would get the wrong idea about them and that they would not be treated in full accordance with the rules of war.

Actually, this really happened to a German who was captured in a trench on the Somme in 1916. He had in his possession several women's dresses and some dancing slippers. But they were very nice to him.

There were artists of a different type at St Martin's Camp, Boulogne, in 1918. Base camps like that were fearful places earlier in the war, with harsh discipline and endless training and parades. George Weeks remembered St Martin's Camp as a terrible place in 1917. Foul-mouthed corporals harried and chastised him all over the place. But when RSM Key of the Royal Fusiliers arrived there near the end of the war, he found that the men had removed the regimental tags off their tunics and had gone into hiding. When a parade for men of the 3rd and 18th Divisions was called, only those of the 37th and 47th were apparently available. But on the following day, when the 37th and the 47th were due on parade, all available personnel were in the 3rd and 18th Divisions.

King George V visited the Western Front on a regular basis. On one occasion he was inspecting some incinerators. Sadly, one of them had run out of rubbish to burn and was in danger of not being able to show the king how it worked. A bright spark ordered a large bundle of brand new uniforms to be put to special use. Petrol was flung over them and they were set alight.

The king surveyed this blaze: he was no fool. 'Those trousers still have their creases,' he observed.

'They are dangerously infected, Your Majesty,' the CO informed him creatively. But this did not deter His Majesty from taking a closer look at the conflagration.

'Look out, please, sir. Do look out, sir,' warned a now desperate CO, and respectfully dragged his monarch back from the flames. 'They're full of lice!'

The major was later awarded a medal for ingenuity and then sent back to base camp charged with incompetence.

A battalion of the Artists' Rifles was resting in a pretty village on the River Scarpe, west of Arras, in the summer of 1917. They were due back at the front and Corps Command was anxious that they should be ready for the fray. This meant very boring and repetitive manoeuvres and arms drills. However, the Artists largely co-operated because they felt rather sorry for their elderly and totally incompetent CO. He was kind, gentle and decent, but out of his depth. He was a store manager before he volunteered.

But the Artists were really fed up with playing soldiers and they all hid behind a long, tall hedge. 'Penny! Penny! Where's the battalion?' the old buffer called plaintively to his adjutant. It became a catchphrase for the Artists. At any dull moment someone could imitate the poor old major and call out, 'Penny, Penny, where's the battalion?'

Private Stephen Graham's platoon sergeant asked him whether it was true he was a *Times* journalist before the war. 'Yes, that's right,' replied Graham.

'I sent two jokes to "Answers" last week,' the sergeant informed him proudly. (*Answers* was a popular weekly comic for adults.)

'Then we are colleagues and fellow workers,' Graham congratulated him, and thus secured a long-term working understanding with the NCO.

Lieutenant Edwin Vaughan was also an 'artist'. He found a pile of German stick bombs by the ventilator shaft to his dugout. He unscrewed the detonator from one of them and extracted the fuse. It burnt for about five seconds, the popping noises growing louder and louder. His colleagues were at the bottom of the shaft. He put his ear to the ground in the hope of picking up their reactions. 'Good God!' exclaimed Lieutenant Ewing to Lieutenant Teague.

'Blinking good job it was a dud,' said his relieved companion. Whereupon Vaughan de-detonated six more bombs and dropped them into the hole. One of them actually hit Ewing. When they had picked themselves up Teague pointed out: 'They can't all be duds.'

Suddenly Ewing became very alarmed. 'They're gas! Can ye no smell them?' Vaughan heard them scrabbling around frenziedly for their masks. He jumped into the trench and met them as they tumbled out of the dugout. 'Hello,' he greeted them merrily, 'have you joined the Ku-Klux-Klan?'

'Put on your mask, ye fule!' yelled Ewing. 'The air's full o' gas.' He coughed up the 'gas' which had got into his lungs. Vaughan winked at Teague and Teague understood and winked back. They loved ragging a rather sombre Ewing.

Discipline

Relationships with commanding officers could often be strained. The 10/DLI was resting peacefully near Albert when their (reasonable) lieutenant-colonel was promoted and the DLI (sometimes referred to as the 'Devil's Last Issue') were aghast to learn that they were getting back the previous CO, who, according to Ernest Parker, had returned from 'being a town major or some similar rest cure'.

True to form, the 'town major' decided that the 10/DLI, to a man, needed haircuts. However, no army barbers were available so the blighter ordered the next best thing – 'Army clippers, heads for the shearing of'. Senior NCOs got the unenviable task of clipping the locks of their companies. There were a lot of barnets to get through so they were in a bit of a hurry – no time for finesse. The result was multiple bleeding heads. Sergeant Matty Parker was so disgusted by the annihilation of his wavy locks that he borrowed some clippers and cut a deep crescent out of his depleted glory, licked his purple pencil and inscribed his name, number and rank on his skull, plus a memorandum to his CO.

The Military Police attached to the 10/DLI had their own problems with these sturdy men. One of their corporals, assisted by a private, had the thankless task of turfing drunks out of an *estaminet*. The corporal gave last-minute instructions. 'I'll throw 'em out and you count 'em,' he ordered. The private waited patiently by the door, also licking his purple pencil in readiness. The first 'customer' came flying out and the dutiful private was just about to write 'one' when the hurtling figure spoke: 'Don't start counting yet. It's me,' it advised. 'It' was the corporal.

The 2/20 Londons were in the St Eloi trenches in the autumn of 1916. Their CO slithered along the duckboards in pitch darkness and heavy rain. He was a little man completely shrouded in a voluminous mackintosh. A visiting Canadian sapper stood aside to let him pass and jammed his leg down a slimy sump hole. 'I'm sorry, my man,' said the lieutenant-colonel kindly. 'Are you all right?'

The engineer didn't have a clue who the little fellow was. 'Okay, old cock,' he responded cheerfully, dragged his leg free and hurried on his way. The CO was momentarily speechless, but soon recovered. 'Stop that man,' he ordered Londoners standing around. 'Stop him, I say.' Never in his life had he been addressed as 'old cock'. The soldiers tried to obey but only half-heartedly; they didn't really want to apprehend anyone who had called their colonel 'old cock' so they 'failed' to find him and bring him back. There could be months of fun in recounting the tale of how an other rank had called the CO 'old cock'.

In the summer of 1915, having newly arrived in the Ypres Salient with the Royal Horse Artillery, 2nd Lieutenant Julian Tyndale-Biscoe was short of revolver practice and, glancing around a ruined farm, he spotted the picture of a saint; it was a perfect target. As he blazed away, a Roman Catholic divisional padre, of all people, chanced by and roundly rebuked Tyndale-Biscoe for his sacrilege. But the young subaltern was very chipper and told the padre to mind his own business. The chaplain, taking offence, reported him to the general, who reported him to the RHA colonel, who reported him to the adjutant, who reported him to Julian's company commander, whom Tyndale-Biscoe told to get lost.

When Jerry first used poison gas in 1915, the BEF had to hurriedly find some protection for the PBI (Poor Bloody Infantry). Early devices were somewhat primitive. The first was simply a cotton pad wrapped in gauze which was soaked in a soda compound when a gas attack was signalled. They carried the soda around in a bottle. But instructions for its use did not apparently filter down to every

Tommy because a Fusilier in the 2/RWF (May 1915) drank it. In addition to not feeling very well he was also put on a charge, adding insult to injury.

Exposure

Lieutenant Eberle had a very successful sapper's war, rising to the rank of lieutenant-colonel. As noted before, he was closely involved with the development of the 'Bungalore Torpedo', designed to destroy enemy wire. Gathered in a field with very senior officers, the subaltern had to explain the intricacies of the igniter for the torpedo. A crowd of interested onlookers watched proceedings from afar. One Fusilier had a clear opinion about what was going on: 'A f***ing fine thing I calls it when a f***ing Corpse [sic] Commander 'as to come and learn 'ow to fight from a f***ing Lootenant.'

Young Lieutenant Easton was billeted on a farm at Busnes and wanted a bath badly. But he was hoping for something a bit more civilised than a zinc container placed in the midden. The daughter of the house filled it with hot water and retired to observe events from the kitchen window. Easton's servant managed to get a towel around his officer to preserve modesty but the officer was perturbed when the farmer's wife popped out, picked up his clothes and took them away to be washed. It was good service but as Easton gave himself a rapid scrub (when he had been looking forward to a long soak), he was thinking desperately how to leap into the towel without revealing anything of a vital nature.

As he performed these clumsy manoeuvres the daughter observed to one of Easton's fellow officers: '*C'est un drôle, ça*' (*drôle* = funny-peculiar).

Whilst travelling in box trucks ('Hommes 40, Chevaux 8') from Boulogne to Mailley-Maillet on the Somme battlefield, in March 1917, the 24/Queen's were allowed to remove their boots for the duration of the journey. George Weeks wrote in his memoirs:

Unfortunately, the boots got mixed up, with dire results. I was one of the unlucky ones with a size nine and one about size seven. The next camp *was some two miles from the railhead and I among a dozen others had to march to this place wearing only one boot ... the men wearing larger boots than their size were booked for fatigues.*

Possibly, German High Command, on hearing this news, congratulated itself that the war would easily be won if enemy troops were marching up to the line clad in only one boot.

Horace Bruckshaw (Royal Naval Division) noted that on 5 August 1916 a fellow jack tar was provided with a new pair of trousers – quite an event. His old ones were really falling to pieces so he took them along to the incinerator and left them to be destroyed. However, he had taken Bruckshaw's trousers by mistake, and by the time they rushed out to try and save them they were gone and replaced with trousers in a worse state than Bruckshaw's. Who finally got the new pair is anybody's guess.

Strange Ones

Residing at Vlamertinghe near Ypres in 1915 were two incredibly decrepit crones living in an equally dilapidated cottage a few hundred metres from the front line. All other civilians in the vicinity had long since gone, but these two simply had nowhere to go, and in any case, they were making a fortune selling coffee to the artillery. The recoil from the big guns, nevertheless, was slowly dismantling the cottage and it became a race between the old dames getting enough money to buy somewhere else to live and the final demolition of their abode. Meanwhile, the coffee was excellent as the gunners kept them supplied with the best they could buy from the ramparts in Ypres.

Another visit by King George V, this time to St Pol, was planned for 18 August 1916, but it had to be very hush-hush for obvious reasons. Only very senior staff officers were informed of the plan and communications about it were exchanged in a complex secret code. On the 17th, however, the town crier of St Pol proudly paraded around the streets of his town beating his drum and crying out: '*Oyez! Oyez! Citoyens de St Pol, Le Roi d'Angleterre est arrivé à St Pol! Vive le Roi!*'

Lieutenant Mottram, whom you may recall had the task of settling claims for compensation from Flemish citizens, went out one day to investigate a claim from the owner of a 'crazy old pub' that soldiers had not paid for eggs or chickens, or both. Mottram asked the proprietor if he could identify the regiment these soldiers belonged to and the scruffy devil produced a piece of sacking with a flourish, declaring that this identified the regiment without a doubt. Mottram carefully inspected the fragment and found the letters O.A.T.S. stencilled upon it. He remained calm and finally decided that there were ten chickens before the O.A.T.S. arrived and none when they left. He settled for 10 francs and a very nice dinner washed down by some decent wine.

Lieutenant Harry Collins of the Coldstream Guards was something of a character but encountered grave difficulties in getting out of bed in the dark mornings. He ordered his long-suffering servant to wake him at the appropriate time. The batman dutifully shook Collins at the appointed hour and the officer sat bolt upright and screamed at his man for being, 'A barstard and a son-of-a-bitch'. Later, Collins apologised to the servant and asked him to wake him again the following morning. He did and got called 'A barstard and a son-of-a-bitch'. It happened every morning: it was a successful system.

On the third day of the retreat from Mons, in August 1914, a staff officer's servant turned to him and said: 'I suppose we'll catch them up eventually, sir.'

A private in the Artists' Rifles had been a music hall performer and apparently his most significant role to date had included the line, 'Is Mrs May hin?' which he repeated again and again ad nauseam, thoroughly getting on everybody's nerves, which were already frayed following their arrival at the Gavrelle front line in the summer of 1917. One night he was out in no-man's-land repairing the barbed wire when he spotted what had been reported as an ex-German machine gun post. He couldn't resist the challenge: he stuck his head inside the entrance and called out, 'Is Mrs May hin?'

On this occasion Mrs May was 'hin'. He fled precipitately as Jerries poured out of the dugout. He was shot in the heel. He reported to the aid post and was given a Blighty One – a most satisfactory conclusion for everybody concerned.

Spies

At no other time in the war was talk of spies as rife as during the retreat from Mons in 1914, when it was comparatively simple for an English-speaking German to infiltrate the fleeing BEF. James Jack's French liaison officer and interpreter, Captain Raoul Duval, was arrested on suspicion of being a spy on 31 August. Jack intervened to secure his release but Duval was still furious and demanded to know the name of the arresting officer in order to arrange a duel after the war. Jack, doing his best to prevent an international incident, pretended to go over to the officer and ask for his name. He returned to Duval and announced: 'He is Lieutenant Smith of Stepney.'

'Then I shall be in touch with Lieutenant Smith of Stepney,' promised Duval. He was not able to fulfil the challenge: he was killed at Verdun in 1916.

Jack himself and a fellow officer were stopped on 5 October 1914 and accused of being spies fiendishly disguised as British officers. Their chauffeur saved the day by using the sort of English swear

An observation post in a dummy tree on Hill 63 during the Battle of Messines, June 1917.

words that proved he was English – a four-lettered invitation for the accuser to go away, doubt on his parentage, plus another four-letter word and a reference to the bloke's backside.

Even during the advance from the Marne to the Aisne in September 1914 there were alarms about 'spies'. A dispatch rider in Jack's battalion (1/Cameron Highlanders) was arrested because he was asking questions, was unshaven, dirty and oil-stained and 'did not look British'. The poor bloke had been dashing about non-stop for two days delivering messages. Captain Jack rescued him.

The CO and the MO of the 2/RWF were riding into Armentières when they were challenged by diligent sentries of the 5/Scottish Rifles. The colonel complimented them on their efficiency and warned them that there were some suspicious-looking officers following them into the town. They knew full well that their adjutant and company commanders were coming along behind, looking forward to a nice evening in town. 'I'd pick them up if I were you,' suggested the MO.

'Yes, sir,' responded a sergeant smartly. 'We'll take care of them, never you mind, sir.'

Another colonel – W.N. Nicholson, attached to a Highland division – was challenged by another Scottish sentry in the trenches for the current password. Nicholson knew it was a Scottish town but couldn't quite remember which one. 'Dundee,' he hazarded.

'You're wrong, man,' said the sentry. 'It's Aberdeen.'

Training & Recruitment

Officers and other ranks sometimes attended courses to expand their range of skills. There were four signallers at Quesnoy-sur-Airaines in May 1918. Any course member found guilty of misconduct was sent straight back to their unit. A Dublin Fusilier was apprehended in an *estaminet*-cum-shop after midnight. 'Sure an' oi came in for a rubber for the morning,' he explained. Fumes of *vin blanc* emanated from his person as he spoke and his pockets were crammed full of more bottles of the stuff.

By October 1918 recruits to the 1/15 Londons (or Civil Service Rifles) were becoming a mixed bag, to say the least. Two arrived on

Major-General (*addressing the men before practising an attack behind the lines*): I want you to understand that there is a difference between a rehearsal and the real thing. There are three essential differences: First, the absence of the enemy. Now (*turning to the Regimental Sergeant-Major*) What is the second difference? Sergeant-Major: The absence of the General, Sir.

Cartoon by Claude Shepperson.

the 8th – an Italian organ-grinder, who could not understand English, and a violinist from the Imperial Russian Ballet. The latter was placed in the regimental band, but the organ-grinder couldn't be suited in the same way because the band didn't possess an organ.

When the tunnelling companies were searching for recruits in October 1916, both the 2/RWF and the 2/West Yorkshires were keen to volunteer en masse because double rations were on offer for a 'hush-hush' job. The 17/West Yorkshires also took the bait despite being a Bantam Battalion, all standing about 5 feet nothing. Little did they know that they were set to join huge New Zealand tunnellers working twenty-four-hour shifts below ground. The Bantams who were employed certainly earned their double rations. It would have been interesting to see them digging alongside the colonial giants.

By August 1917 there was a severe shortage of officers and the brigadier kept sending increasingly desperate pleas to battalion commanders to name possible candidates for officer training. The CO had made this plea for the fourth time in a week on 8 August and in exasperation forwarded the names of all his sanitary orderlies, all veterans of the Boer War.

Scroungers & Souvenir-Hunters

Privates Purkiss and Kiddell of the 2/West Yorkshires had exceptional scrounging skills, and were outstanding for the craft even in a regiment crammed with such experts. Sidney Rogerson had the dubious honour of being their company commander. When they reached Camp 34 on the Somme battlefield on 7 November 1916, Lieutenant-Colonel Jack called his company commanders together for a conference. Before he got going he congratulated Rogerson on the scrounging skills of his men. They had been in the area for only a few minutes and yet Jack's very nice stove had already disappeared.

But that was nothing compared to Purkiss and Kiddell's feat of purloining a huge balloon tarpaulin from another battalion in Camp 34, big enough to cover half a company. Obviously it was

Private John Hines, the 'Souvenir King', at Polygon Wood, September 1917.

not wise to use it whilst in the camp, but just concealing it from the rightful owners required felonious skill of the first order.

Lieutenant Easton's Fusilier company was in Embrey and doing quite well for apples because a friendly local farmer shook a tree for them in his orchard every night. But another company sniffed apples and two whole trees were stripped under cover of darkness. As a consequence, the farmer refused to shake any more trees. Easton and his men were very put out by this travesty and, in the hope of persuading the farmer to change his mind, placed a night guard in the orchard. A messenger from the Middlesex Regiment came across the orchard during the night and took an apple. He was apprehended by the apple watch.

Unfortunately, this runner was carrying an important communiqué from brigade to division. Following the non-appearance of the messenger, division sent a runner to brigade asking where he was with the information they needed. Brigade sent another messenger with the message that they had already sent a runner with the information. After a few enquiries the original runner was found trussed up in a wine cellar. Luckily, both brigade and division thought this was a hoot.

At Foncquevillers in January 1916, a departing transport officer took with him a rather attractive sculptured metal weather vane from the roof of a brasserie as a souvenir. The vane depicted a farmer trundling a wheelbarrow. It was punctured by a lot of bullet holes. But it had proved useful in showing wind direction – particularly handy in the event of a gas attack. The CO of the relieving battalion was annoyed at the disappearance of the vane and sent a stiff note to the CO of the relieved battalion. A message was sent along to the transport officer; but he was quite attached to this piece of sculpture and cut a replica from a large tin, adding authentic-looking holes. He brought it back to Foncquevillers and apologised profusely to the lieutenant-colonel now in residence, who was very smug about his triumph in getting the vane back. In fact, he was so elated he gave the transport officer a drink and said there were no hard feelings.

A German sniper at Cuinchy drilled a neat hole in Robert Graves' periscope (May 1916). Graves sent it home to his mother as a souvenir but she took it along to the manufacturers and demanded a replacement. Amazingly, they coughed up, probably because of her blatant cheek. She sent it out to her son.

More Sandbags to Fill

There were actually 'Sandbag Clubs' at home. One of these clubs sent to Guy Chapman's company some beautifully stitched bags; ironic when you think of the hundreds of thousands of bags wrapped round the soldiers (as well, of course, as the millions on trench parapets). Chapman's company put these ornate bags to very good use – a dugout was roofed with some nice orange and red samples. A charming black pair kept Chapman's boots from scratching his head when used as a pillow.

Lieutenant Tyndale-Biscoe of the Royal Horse Artillery (Commines Canal, September 1915) was contacted by the 'Sewing Party' of Godalming in Surrey. What did they need? He replied that they were short of sandbags so these gallant ladies supplied 8,000 of them. Sadly, they were stolen during transit.

Lieutenant Eberle sent home some unwanted belongings in a sandbag from Foncquevillers (January 1916). His mother returned the bag washed and ironed. Eberle calculated that during the previous three weeks he had issued 130,000 bags. He still had 60,000 in stock.

Fizzers

The 2/RWF were well supplied with dodgy characters. Take 'Broncho', for instance, up before the CO for the umpteenth time in November 1914. He was given twenty-eight days of Field Punishment No 1 and the lieutenant-colonel also warned Broncho that if he appeared before him again the scoundrel would be shot. Broncho bravely pointed out that the CO had already threatened him with execution after his previous 'crime' – in fact, the three previous times – and the lieutenant-colonel told him to clear off or he'd shoot Broncho on the spot himself.

'Fizzer' Green also made frequent appearances. One of them followed Fizzer's headlong descent into a ditch when marching up to the front (March 1915). There was a suspicion that he was very drunk at the time. He could be executed for being drunk on the way up to the front line. But Fizzer did not need a defence counsel to mount a case. He explained to the CO that his family suffered a genetic weakness of the knees which could strike them down at any moment. Indeed, an uncle had been run down by a horse tram in Barking after his knees gave way. This was what propelled Fizzer into the ditch. By now even the lieutenant-colonel was convulsed with laughter and could hardly speak to give Fizzer twenty-eight days' No 1. Fizzer was very pleased with his powerful and creative defence.

Get Well Soon

Lieutenant Mottram was in the Base Hospital in Boulogne for treatment in 1915. The man in the next bed had a case of the DTs, gripped by hallucinations. He told Mottram that there was a black man and a retriever sitting on his bed. A medical orderly ushered in an elegant lady attired in fashionable furs, hurriedly summoned from England. However, she stood at the foot of the bed and stared silently at the patient. The impact of her presence on him was electrifying: he shrieked and screamed for a full minute and then crawled under the bedclothes shaking like a leaf.

Lieutenant Slack (4/East Yorkshires) was in hospital on 18 October 1917 when he was visited by a Wesleyan padre. But this man of God appeared to be unversed in the arts of visiting patients in hospital. 'How are you?' he asked, and Slack said he was progressing well, and that was it. The minister obviously had not written a script beyond 'How are you?' He just sat and stared at Slack.

Slack had good manners: he couldn't just ignore the chap and go on reading his newspaper, so he attempted to prime him with a series of questions of his own. But the only replies he got were 'yes', 'no', 'I think so' and 'perhaps'. Slack picked up his paper and the visitor evaporated.

The 12/Argyll and Sutherland Highlanders had captured some very deep German latrines and Captain D. Dick discovered one of his men floundering around in the enemy excreta. 'What are you doing, man?' called the rather bewildered officer.

'Getting my tunic, sir. It fell in, sir,' explained the soldier.

'Come out, man. I'll get you another tunic. God knows what sort of diseases there are down there.'

An advert for a bullet-proof vest. Private Andrew Bowie later discovered that it was no good.

'Ah, but sir, my moothie is in the pocket. You won't get me another moothie like this one, sir. I don't feel all that well, though, sir.' (A 'moothie' was a mouth organ.)

Alfred Burrage was on his way to Le Havre in March 1917 and the Channel was a bit choppy. A lot of the men were seasick – some very ill. One bloke had a prolonged seizure, a rather disgusting gargling and snarling attempt to vomit. A pal called out: 'Still got your teeth, Jack, mate?'

Sickness struck down many a Tommy. Burrage himself caught trench fever in May 1917 without going near a trench. Sergeant Britcher of the Royal Engineers Signals Company, 34th Division, claimed that the lump on his face was making him go deaf. In an *estaminet* one night a cheeky private asked him if he would like a drink. Britcher glared round at the offender and remarked: 'It ain't no good you saying would you like a drink 'cos I can't hear you, can I, what with the tumour!'

Lance-Corporal Vic Cole of the 7/Queen's Own was wounded on the Somme in June 1916 as the impending battle loomed. But he seemed unlikely to get a Blighty One so he chewed on a piece of cordite, producing the symptoms of a heart attack and was sent to England before the big battle began.

A convenient sickness was never far from the thoughts of Tommies. Lieutenant Graham H. Greenwell of the 1/4 Oxon and Bucks Light Infantry recalled that men in his company paid two shillings and sixpence (a third of a week's pay for most men) for the privilege of sleeping next to a man who looked like he was going down with measles ('Plugstreet' Wood, 27 May 1915).

In the Court Circular in *The Times*, for 5 August 1916, Captain Robert Graves of the Royal Welch Fusiliers declared that a previous announcement that he was dead was premature. He was, in fact, recovering from his wounds at the Queen Alexandra Hospital in Highgate, north London. However, Cox's Bank continued to regard Graves as dead and he had great difficulty in getting his cheques accepted.

The commander of the 19th (Western) Division went to hospital to visit one of his colonels, who had been wounded in the neck. He was ushered into the presence of a grey-haired officer. 'This is not my colonel,' declared the general.

'Oh yes, it is,' insisted the Sister smartly, 'but the colonel has run out of hair dye.'

It was 21 April 1918 and the British Army was still reeling from the German offensive. The MO of the 2/RWF was lucky to have a reasonable aid post, not easy in the conditions of retreat. However, it was not the Jerries who caused the death of an orderly, but a dodgy burner in the cellar. He was, in fact, the doctor's servant. He was pronounced as deceased from the effects of carbon monoxide poisoning. He was wrapped in blankets (he would be charged for them, as corpses were) and placed outside the aid post (not a good advertisement for wounded men arriving for treatment), but a fresh wind blew up from the east and the 'corpse' came to life and started snoring loudly.

Deserving of Medals

Medals abounded on the Western Front. Driver Alfred Henn of the 3rd Battery of the Royal Horse Artillery was taking ammunition up to the front line along with two fellow gunners. What they were driving were mules but shelling commenced and Alfred's mate, Horace, abandoned the mules and jumped into a trench. As he went past, one of the mules kicked him in the face. When they arrived back at the battery, Alfred said that Horace had shown conspicuous bravery in continuing to bring up the ammunition despite being wounded by a fragment from a 'Minniewerfer' (German mine). Horace was thus awarded the Military Medal.

Some men, of course, actually deserved a medal. On 24 July 1916 a corporal was quizzed by an officer he did not know at Bully Crater. This interrogation seemed excessive – more than an officer from another regiment would need to know. So the corporal became suspicious. 'Hands up,' he ordered tersely, and pointed his wire cutters at this possible German spy. 'Who are you and why do you need all this information?'

The officer put up his hands even though he was armed with a revolver. He provided his name, number and rank and commended the corporal for his vigilance. But the latter doggedly kept the wire cutters under the strange officer's nose and turned to another form of interrogation. 'Who won the cup last year?' he demanded.

Bombardier J.W. Palmer was laying out wires for signals during the Battle of Loos, in September 1915, near the Hohenzollern Redoubt, a formidable enemy fortification. Palmer had been told to lay the wires right up to the Hulluch crossroads. But an officer stopped him. 'Where you going?' he demanded.

'Hulluch crossroads, sir.'

'You'd better bugger off back – we haven't captured the bloody Hulluch crossroads yet.'

Honour Satisfied

Lieutenant Eberle and other corps engineers were miffed to be told by the chief Royal Engineer that they had failed to observe a house being used by the Germans in no-man's-land (Ploegsteert Wood, June 1915). The CRE had been given this piece of intelligence by a rather jubilant staff major, glad to put one over on the sappers.

'Was,' the CRE requested, 'this house occupied by the Germans at night?' (Or, in other words, 'Have you cocked up, you cocky Engineers?') So Eberle and another sapper went out at night to find this 'house'. What they found was a heap of rubble in a hole hidden by tall grass, with a shuttered door lying on top of it. They reported this to the CRE but the major wouldn't let it rest there and ordered all periscopes along a quarter of a mile of trench to focus their attention on the 'house'. All officers, NCOs and sentries were ordered to watch it day and night. But absolutely no movement was detected: the honour of the Royal Engineers was upheld. The incident also provided them with endless opportunities to rib the major with references to the 'lost house'.

The Royal Fusiliers were at rest in Doullens (Somme) in 1916 when in the cookhouse the mess waiter called the mess cook a bastard; not a clever thing to do when surrounded by lots of knives. As a matter of honour the cook stabbed the waiter with a carving knife. The military court accepted that this was an affair of honour and the cook was sentenced to just fourteen days' Field Punishment No 1. However, instead of being tied to a fence or wagon wheel for several hours every day, the cook was allowed to do extra duties in his own mess. Meanwhile, men scared witless by incessant shelling, bombing and shooting were executed.

EIGHT

Sex

Main Chance

Leave home was not properly organised until well into 1915 and so large numbers of married officers and men did not see their wives for a long time. A common reason given in applications for leave was 'acute sexual starvation'. Lieutenant Brian Frayling of the 171 Tunnelling Company observed in February 1915 that accepting this as a valid reason for leave would have almost emptied the Western Front. Frayling also pointed out that these regular soldiers of the original BEF, and similar reinforcements from overseas stations, in 1915 were renowned for their sexual activity – whether in marriage or not he did not say. He also recalled the recruitment of tough Durham coalminers to the tunnelling companies early in 1915. Up in front of the MO of 171 Company, one of them was asked: 'Have you been circumcised?'

'Oh, no sir,' replied the miner. 'That's just fair wear and tear.'

However, Kitchener volunteers were just as keen. When 2/Queen's marched up through Boulogne on 2 June 1915 they were highly interested to see hordes of young ladies lining the streets to greet them. The Tommies, away from their families, felt uninhibited and gave vent to 'franglais': 'Vou jig-a-jig avec moi tonight ma chèrie?' they called out exuberantly. Their cheek was met with screams of laughter and perhaps delight from the girls (and older ladies). 'Tommie! Tommie!' they yelled, and threw biscuits and chocolates.

Yet by Christmas 1916, at least, these exchanges had become more sedate. As the 8/Leicesters left Béthune they asked rather dutifully: '*Voulez-vous coucher avec moi ce soir?*'

'*Àpres la guerre*,' was the standard reply by this time – and no biscuits or chocolates either.

Nevertheless, British soldiers, married or not, found themselves able to say things to French and Flemish girls they would not have dared to say to English girls. They must have got a real thrill out of hearing these foreign ladies repeat all sorts of obscenities – often without a clue as to what they meant.

Pictures

Trench journals also did their bit to try and relieve sexual frustration, although *The Wipers Times* was restrained, pointing out that 'This is a family journal. Ed.' It did ask, however, on 20 March 1916, 'Who leads in Kirchner collections?' These were pictures of scantily clad females. Lieutenant Vaughan (1/8 Warwickshires) had a portable assembly of 'Harrison Fisher' girls. Some of these postcards, in deference to Bruce Bairnsfather's famous cartoon, were captioned: 'If you knows of a better 'ole.'

The 8/Leicesters in a Berles-au-Bois billet in 1915 remembered the walls being plastered with very professional crayon and pencil drawings of nude and semi-nude girls.

Opportunities

But there were opportunities for the real thing; sometimes it was not clear whether these were 'professional' services or not. Sam, a private in the Monmouths, was regarded as the ugliest man you could see, but he had formed an 'arrangement' with 'a lady up the hill'. If the old man was out she put some washing on the clothes line. Other ladies in the vicinity had copied this habit: notices were put in windows,

'Washing done for soldiers'. Whether other services were on offer only genuine customers could find out.

The 8/Leicesters, training near Doullens in May 1916, got wind of another 'lady' who was available for a consideration. It was a nice evening so a small party of Leicesters tramped to the venue indicated. Only a couple of them were serious punters, the rest were keeping them company just for a laugh. They got it: after prolonged knocking on the front door an upstairs window was flung open and the lady poured down a torrent of abuse on the Tommies. Undeterred, they resumed their assault on the door; the window was flung open once more and the lady reappeared with a chamber pot thrust in front of her. She tipped the lot over their upturned faces and they stumbled back to the billet helpless with laughter and covered in sweet violets.

The batman for the RSM of the 2/RWF was much more successful. Everyone knew him as 'Nutty'. In billets 5 miles behind the Cambrai front he was enjoying a fruitful evening. However, at a critical moment, the Germans started shelling. '*Oh, M'sieu Nutty,*' exclaimed his companion. '*Allemagne beaucoup bombard.*'

Nutty was extensively put out by this interruption by the war but was determined to proceed. 'Yes, and in a minute M'sieu Nutty boko bombard, too.'

A Welsh Guardsman was spotted running away from a pig sty attired only in a shirt flapping round his bare backside. The farmer was duly informed by 'friends' of the Guardsman that he was having sex with one of his pigs. Nobody noticed the two daughters of the farmer fleeing in another direction.

A sergeant of the 1/9 King's Liverpool revealed to Private Dick Trafford (late in 1916) that he was determined to 'go over the plonk' (parapet) and get killed because he was sure he was suffering from venereal disease. The thought of his wife finding out about his condition was too much to bear. He figured out that if he was killed his wife would at least get a pension, which was better than the humiliation of knowing that her husband was unfaithful. He was killed the next day. This item hasn't an iota of humour in it.

The Kemmel Times (with which was incorporated *The Wipers Times* and *The New Church Times*) for 3 July 1916 had the familiar section on 'things we want to know'. The journal was curious as to whether 'Tina's knowledge of troop movements was more profitable than her canteen'.

Alfred Burrage and 'Dave Barney' of the Artists' Rifles reached a village on the River Scarpe near Arras in September 1917 and encountered a plump lady standing outside her *estaminet*. Some of her ample proportions were due to the fact that she was pregnant. 'Souvenir Canadien,' she revealed, rather proudly.

Edwin Vaughan (1/8 Warwickshires) was in the Hôtel du Commerce in Arraines-sur-Somme, on 16 January 1916, for a drink and some company. A female appeared; she was coarse, stout and was dressed in a filthy and torn black skirt, a woollen bodice and red shoes, through which black, much-darned stockinged toes protruded. Her face was thickly covered in powder to hide a mass of purple pimples. Her right hand was bandaged and held in front of her bodice. She tripped in with girlish mien and mincing steps whilst *Un Peu d'Amour* was tinkled on a tinny piano. She skittishly approached the young Vaughan with a horrid leer and lisped, 'I loff you', and evil-smelling breath swept over the subaltern.

Paying For It

J.B. Priestley had a similar experience. At the end of the war he was working as a variety agent in the Labour Corps depot in Rouen. He went out for a stroll one day and encountered a hobbling crone. Priestley politely wished her '*Bonjour*', and she, grinning hideously and toothlessly, handed him a piece of paper. It was a licence entitling her to be a prostitute. In fluently bad French Priestley explained that he wasn't in the mood.

Cities and towns had their brothels. One, in the Rue de Gallennes in Le Havre, featured a prostitute who dressed up as a British captain. She couldn't keep up with demand (March 1917).

An *estaminet* in Armentières doubled as a house of ill-repute at 5 francs a time (1915). Sergeant George Ashworth of 2/Lancashire Fusiliers didn't join the queue of men on the stairs, being content with egg and chips and plonk. Upstairs, according to eye witnesses, the girls grabbed your 5-franc note and then checked for signs of venereal disease. Following business, mixed herbs were dipped in boiling water and applied to the strategic body parts as a further precaution. In Paris, apparently, higher-class professionals used a brown powder for the same purpose and there were occasionally unfortunate results. A sergeant of the Monmouths returned from a stint in the city and explained away his injured member by declaring that he had fallen asleep in front of a blazing fire.

In December 1915 the 6/Queen's were at rest in Béthune. When the red lamp was fixed to the door dead on 6 p.m. a line of about 150 men waited patiently outside it. Arrangements inside were supervised by bulky men in red and black hooped jerseys, all of whom had flowing black moustaches and hair plastered down with thick grease. They shoved the customers into line at the foot of the stairs. The women were jaded and worn out – no surprise there. Some were old enough to be grandmas and probably were. Madame-in-charge, the possessor of an enormous bosom, held out her hand for 2 francs per man, one for her and one for the 'girl'.

A brothel in Calais in October 1916 also had queues of 150 or thereabouts, according to John Ellis. The women in the house served a whole battalion a week until they were worn out. The assistant provost-marshal calculated that the usual limit was about three weeks, after which the lady concerned retired to live on her earnings, 'pale but proud'.

Back in Paris, Private W. Luff (1/Queen's) attended a parade on Bastille Day, 1918, and then enjoyed three days' leave in the capital. He finished up in the packed local guardroom like a lot of men, for one reason or another. To Private Luff it seemed that most of them were Scots who had lost their kilts and were wearing frocks.

Postscripts

It was a popular saying throughout the larger part of the war that the army could do anything to you except get you in the family way, but all that changed when the Women's Auxiliary Army Corps (WAAC) turned up on the scene in the last year of the war. By 1918 also,

Amiens had developed in certain directions. The city, it was often said, was full of homosexual officers and Australian deserters – not necessarily the same men. The following was overheard from the lips of a 'pretty' subaltern: 'You've no idea what a long time it takes to brush off this chalk from a black silk dress.'

Anthony French recalled the arrival of his battalion at a large farm dominated by a huge cesspool and an equally mountainous dunghill. The Tommies were happy that the long day's march was over; they were in a jolly mood. The farmer's wife was spotted at the kitchen door and there were hopes of some younger females in residence. 'Bring on the dancing belles,' someone called to Madame. The skittish soldiers took up this cry in their hundreds. The more knowledgeable translated it to: '*Les filles de la dance! Ici!*'

'We want the dancing girls!' came a thunderous final flourish.

Madame, surveying them impassively from the doorway, finally muttered, '*Attendez*', and then enigmatically, to an old crone standing in the corner of the midden, '*Marie – Arsene*'.

Whilst Madame strode up to a barn, reached inside and pulled out a cow, Marie toddled off round a corner. The cow was tied to a post in the middle of the yard and Marie reappeared leading an enormous bull, presumably named Arsene, which proceeded to perform its function in life on the cow. For once, the Tommies were struck dumb; they couldn't think what to say as Madame now lectured them on not touching any of her chickens, firmly pointing to the birds.

Weather, Lice & Rats

Not a Picnic

Fighting in the trenches was not a picnic: it was very often bloody. Even on quiet fronts where the combatants had 'understandings' about not firing at one another, or not much and probably at acceptable times and not very accurately, there was still the weather, the lice and the

Lieutenant-Colonel Robertson, 1/Cameron Highlanders, on his rounds, 5 January 1915. From the collection of Major-General R.C. Money.

rats to contend with. If there were, in addition, shells, bullets, mines and bombs, then rain, snow, sleet, the lice crawling all over you and the rats scampering under your feet were even worse.

There were also jobs like going back along the communication trench in the dark (usually about half a mile) and picking up supplies and bringing them back. Other men repaired trenches, wire entanglements, performed sentry duty and went on night patrols into no-man's-land or even raided enemy trenches, slogging about in water-filled crump holes in the dark. You could be soaked to the skin and freezing for days and the lice and the rats seemed to enjoy the bad weather; the lice bit you mercilessly and the rats ate your food or tried to eat you whilst asleep.

Rain & Ice

But, as with everything else, Tommy made jokes about it all. Trench journals joined in the fun, suggesting that German submarines were being sunk along the Menin Road in 1917. Every battalion during the very wet Battle of Passchendaele hoped to be relieved by the Grand

'Is this the way to P.C. Belfort?'
'What d'you take me for? The Harbour Master?'
Cartoon by Cyril Lomax, chaplain to the 8/DLI.

Jock (*in captured trench*): Coom awa' up here, Donal'; it's drier.

Published by kind permission of the family of Bert Thomas.

Fleet. Bruce Bairnsfather admitted in November 1914 that if he didn't mention the weather it was raining. Lieutenant Billy Congreve of the Rifle Brigade had his platoon floating about in sawn-off beer barrels in the flooded trenches of the Ypres Salient in December 1914. Captain Billie Nevill observed one of his sergeants skirting around a traverse (dividing walls across trenches) with a strong breaststroke (April 1915). It was wet in 1914 and 1915, and it carried on being wet, apart from a couple of baking hot summers in which a few men died from heat stroke, mainly on long marches.

Very often it was cold as well as wet. Lieutenant Bolton of the 2/Argyll and Sutherland Highlanders found on his first stint in a trench that his kilt floated up around his waist and later froze. Many Scots abandoned their kilts and replaced them with sandbags, often of very rough texture. It was so wet on 27 August 1916 that a company commander of the 1/8 Warwickshires considered indenting for a waterwing for each of his men – ninety-six of them. Men with moustaches suffered from icicles drooping down over their mouths. David Bell, a machine-gunner, had this experience on 13 January

1917, and also his bread and cheese froze solid. Quartermaster Sergeant McGregor (8/Black Watch) was philosophical about bad weather. He preferred it raining rain to raining shells. Unfortunately, they sometimes arrived together.

Lice

Optimistic soldiers still clung to the reasonable theory that wet and icy conditions would drown or freeze the lice to death. However, longitudinal and extensive research indicated that these creatures mated more in poor weather, and needed more food. An experiment of this sort was carried out by a Tommy in the 2/West Yorkshires (Citadel Camp, November 1917). He hung out his shirt and pants on a line on a freezing wet night. In the morning, according to him, 'the little barstards were standing on their hind legs and clapping their front feet to keep themselves warm'.

A fed-up soldier of the 7/Royal Warwickshires commented to his equally fed-up pal in April 1915 when he was experiencing his first draft of body invaders: 'It's the little things which are sent to try us. If it was Jerry, you shoots 'im or 'e shoots you, and that's that an' no ill feeling. But these little barstards never lets up.'

Many and varied were the commercial remedies to exterminate the interlopers – powders from many a firm, such as Keating's, a thick cream, or Harrison's 'Pomade', and even 'Vermin in the Trench Lice Belts' from Boots. Every manufacturer, of course, claimed that lice would not be able to live within a mile of their product. Pomade was indeed regarded by Harry Patch as successful because it drove the lice out of the seams and hems up to the neck region where 'you could tweak them off'. What he didn't say was that Pomade was like smearing yourself with thick engine oil and 'victims' sometimes wondered whether they were better off with the lice.

Alfred Burrage of the Artists' Rifles was sent a lice belt in a parcel from a kind auntie. He later reported that the lice loved that belt. It was a home for them, also a nuptial chamber, incubator and nursery. They went for walks on it, mated on it, laid their eggs on it and reared their young on it. The only time they left it was to go and draw their rations.

Visits to the baths in rest areas were another attempted method of execution. Infested clothes were rapidly removed and fumigated. An officer of the 9/Cameron Highlanders, during one of these operations, reckoned he saw a shirt walking unaided across to the fumigator.

Many soldiers became adept at burning out the buggers from seams and hems with fags or matches or lighters. They sat around in convivial groups in dugouts or billets doing this 'chatting' (a 'chat' was a louse). This could prove expensive, with matches and fags often scarce, and there was also the possibility of setting fire to your pants. Candles tended to burn stitches and cause shirt disintegration. There was a long, waxy string which you could buy in army canteens and it wasn't a danger to your clothing. It was cheaper but more tedious to crunch the blighters between finger and nail. There was a rather satisfying little crack as each of the perishers perished.

Arthur Halestrop's mum (he was in the Royal Engineers Signals) swore by the use of Lifebuoy soap. Arthur did as he was told and rubbed it along his seams and he said it was successful. John Reith sprayed a gallon of 'Lysol' over his person, bunk and hut but he didn't announce the result.

The 'de-lousing centres' or baths were often local breweries with a plentiful supply of adapted beer barrels or wine vats, and water. But de-loused bodies and clothes were a paradise for new populations of lice, free from competition for a while. The baths constituted a sort of mart where deals could be struck on your particular and possibly distinctive batch of lice. The 7/Queen's definitely took advantage of a swap shop system: 'I'll give you one of my little ones for one of your big 'uns.'

'Can I be sure that they are genuine trench chats?'

'You have my word on it. Only from the finest eggs and there's plenty more where they came from. If you don't obtain complete satisfaction you can rest assured that when you don someone else's so-called fumigated shirt you can look forward to fresh supplies of the sods.'

Tommies of the 2/West Yorkshires vied with one another to build up the most interesting collections (Somme, November 1916). A mate of Private 'Nobby' Clarke had all known types, except one with pink eyes and revolving teeth.

Lice also gave rise to theoretical debates. Robert Graves in the Auchy trenches (May 1915) was asked for his view on the question, 'Should you kill old or young lice?' One opinion was that if you killed older ones the young would die of grief. On the other hand, if you only dispatched young ones, could you get the elders when they attended the funerals?

Soldiers going on leave had to be certified as not being lousy, but wives and mothers in Blighty were generally confronted by walking pestilences. That was a view recorded in February 1918, so families generally spent the war fighting off invasion.

Private Daniel Sweeney (2/Lincolns) discovered the only true way to get rid of lice on 2 August 1916. He was at a rest camp and went with his mates for a swim in a small stream. All of them were extremely lousy: Sweeney calculated he had at least 1,000 (official researches put the highest count per man at around 350). Quite by chance he deposited his shirt on an ant hill. The ants – after a 'big battle', according to Sweeney – ate all the lice. His chums subsequently also put their shirts on the ant hill with the same rate of success.

Rats

The troops also had serious problems with rats, not only in the trenches but in the rest areas. If the billets were in barns or other outhouses there were swarms of rats everywhere. Trenches and surrounding areas with decaying corpses were even worse. Rats were not fussy about their diet: they ate anything. In the Ypres Salient, Major P.H. Pilditch recounted that the local resident rodents ate everything in their trench mess, including the tablecloth and the operation orders. So he borrowed a large cat and locked it in the mess overnight. In the morning it had simply disappeared – not even a scrap of fur left.

Second Lieutenant C.M. Slack of the 4/East Yorkshires wrote that on 21 April 1916 rats started eating his pipe, a slab of Laesor's chocolate and a candle. A 'favourite' rat of his dwelled in a hole by his bed and at night 'practised the long jump' over Slack's legs and also trained for the 100 yards up and down his body. There were, indeed, other pet rats. Albert was a rest town at the back of the Somme battlefield and was usually referred to by the Tommies as 'Bert'. However, a three-legged, one-eyed rat befriended by Fusiliers near the town in 1917 was afforded the full title of the nearby town and properly called 'Albert'.

A new officer at Cuinchy was awakened from a deep sleep by a violent scuffle in a corner. When he shone his torch there, two rats were fighting over a severed hand.

Rats bit sleeping men: on 2 January 1916 at Foncquevillers it was freezing and an officer of the Royal Engineers, also in a deep sleep (if you only had four or less hours' sleep in twenty-four hours, it was going to be deep), suffered thus. He sat up with bulging eyes, sucking his bleeding hand and swinging his torch with the other, expressing his feelings in the vilest possible language. But rats were oblivious to bad language.

A special detachment of the Artists' Rifles was on its way to guard Field Marshal Haig at Bavincourt, in April 1917, and had a night's stay in a rat-infested barn. The corporal in charge – known as 'Duckboard Bill' because on a previous tour of duty in France he had slipped on a duckboard and earned himself a Blighty One – was a sybarite and had supplied himself with a pneumatic pillow. Not one rat would come near this pillow, for some reason. So, while the other Artists were kept awake by the scampering creatures, Duckboard Bill slept peacefully on. But experiments by the restless men proved that if you shone a torch on a rat it tried to escape from the beam. Further research demonstrated that they were more scared by the beam than the corporal's pillow. The Artists were able, with several torches, to run a veritable swarm of rats over his pillow and over him. He leapt violently to his feet, spitting, choking and cursing.

Rats in the trenches became larger and larger on account of the availability of flesh. One such monster sat on the parapet in front of some men of the 6/Connaught Rangers (1 October 1916). 'Puss! Puss!' they called. Private Thomas McIndoe (12/Middlesex) figured that the rats he saw were so big you could stick two between the shafts of a milk float and do a milk round.

Henry Allingham enjoyed shooting rats front on, creating 'tunnels on four legs' (Hellfire Corner, Ypres, 1917). But Lieutenant Eberle (November 1916) discovered that firing at large rats woke up his fellow officers and turned instead to 'nipper mousetraps'. He snared eight mice and stunned two rats.

Captain F.A. Bean, a medical officer in the Black Watch, sat rather morosely in an infested trench during the Battle of Loos in September 1915. He perked up a bit when he espied in the gloom one of the blighters sitting there, gazing at him. He stealthily removed his revolver, took careful aim and missed. Damn! The creature continued to stare at him. It was almost impossible to frighten off these bloated pests. Well, they were so fat, they couldn't run anyway.

The second time around Captain Bean was determined to get him. He took very careful aim – and missed again! Rising angrily, he rushed at the beast and was about to give it a mighty kick when he perceived that the 'rat' was actually a Mills grenade bomb.

An 'official' notice was issued to soldiers of the 2/RWF in June 1917 to the effect that they were 'advised' that when obliged to stand to attention whilst holding a (presumably dead) rat they should ensure that its tail was in line with the crease on their trousers. Endless fun could be obtained by throwing dead rats at one another in trenches. Particularly amusing was picking one up by the tail and slinging it on to the recumbent form of a comrade trying to get some sleep. It landed with a satisfying 'Thud!'

'Whassit?' the awoken pal would grunt, and you would pretend to be asleep.

Lieutenant William McBride could remember being on Hill 60 (that's how high it was in feet) at the southern end of the Ypres Salient in 1917 when two of his men reported 'creaking' sounds under their feet. Allied and German tunnellers were feverishly engaged in an underground war to undermine each other's positions. Was this the suspected enemy tunnel being driven under Hill 60? McBride sent for tunnelling experts and eventually two ex-Durham coalminers arrived on the scene. They knelt down and each jammed an ear to the ground to investigate the strange sounds. 'Rats,' concluded one of them. 'Aye,' agreed the other, 'f***ing.'

Lieutenant Spicer (2/4 King's Own Yorkshire Light Infantry) found that Harley's 'Rodine' was the most effective rat poison. Rat poison was not issued by the army but apparently some officers and fewer men could afford to buy it, although it hardly made a dent in the rodent population. There were other concoctions: Spicer knew of a 'Something Virus' which had to be mixed with food, but he (at the end of 1915) felt it was not feasible to waste valuable food on vermin so he instructed the sanitary man to mix the stuff with the refuse. It did kill a few rats which had a taste for garbage.

Insects

In a letter to his fiancée of 2 August 1916, Lieutenant Slack (4/East Yorkshires) thanked her for a 'fly smasher'. This had arrived during a prolonged battle with a persistent bluebottle. Captain Billie Nevill remembered thousands of them rising like a blue swarm from the latrines – a useful clue for snipers. Billie chose cheap Woolworth's cigars to asphyxiate them. Slack also had encounters with earwigs. They were particularly fond of his hat. 'Millions' of them filled it up in minutes when he left it on the fire step (27 July 1917).

Letters, Words & Songs

Field Postcards

The most common form of communication home was the field service postcard – army form A2042, also known as a 'Whizz-bang' or 'Quick Firer'. Millions of these were dispatched across the Channel. It was a handy way of telling relatives and friends that you were still alive – just. The printed form had alternative phrases and all the soldier had to do was cross out those that did not apply. For hard-pressed men it was a godsend. For those with limited writing skills it was ideal. It was also a quick way of letting people know if you had been sent to a hospital.

Shown below is an example of a field postcard. This one was

NOTHING is to be written on this side except the date and signature of the sender. Sentences not required may be erased. If anything else is added the post card will be destroyed.

I am quite well.

I have been admitted into hospital
{ sick } and am going on well.
{ wounded } and hope to be discharged soon.

I am being sent down to the base.

I have received your { letter dated_____
{ telegram ,, _____
{ parcel ,, _____

Letter follows at first opportunity.

I have received no letter from you
{ lately.
{ for a long time.

Signature}
only. }

Date_____

[Postage must be prepaid on any letter or post card addressed to the sender of this card.]

(25480) Wt.W3497-293 1,130m. 5/15 M.R.Co.,Ltd.

A sample of a field postcard.

sent home by Private Edward Packe of the 1/Cameron Highlanders early in 1915. It was on show at the Imperial War Museum recently:

{ I am quite well
~~I have been admitted into hospital~~

{ ~~sick~~ } ~~and am going on well~~
{ ~~wounded~~ } ~~and hope to be discharged~~

~~I am being sent down to the base~~

I have received your { letter
~~telegram~~
parcel

Letter follows at first opportunity

~~I have received no letter from you~~ { ~~lately~~
~~for a long time~~

[Packe had received a letter and a parcel but not 'lately'.]

The field postcard was easy prey for comedians and many spoof samples have survived:

I have received your parcel { last week
last month
never

[Trooper Ben Clouting of the 4/Royal Dragoon Guards.]

Below is a tunneller's 'non-standard' 'Whizz-bang' of October 1916. It was not filled in:

I am { pretty well } fed up
{ absolutely }

I have { paid } my mess bill
{ not paid }

I have had no rum { for ..... days }
{ for ..... weeks }

I hope to get leave in 19- { 17
18
19

So this plaintive message could have been sent by someone who had not paid his mess bill, had had no rum for weeks (possibly months) and expected leave in 1919 and was, consequently, absolutely fed up.

Censorship

Letters home were subject to scrutiny for reasons of military security. This was usually the (onerous) task of the company commander – who might have to look through dozens on a daily basis. Officers' letters were also checked. One, received by a wife in Fife in March 1915, suffered terminally in this way. Page 1 had 'Dearest Wife' with the rest scrubbed out. Pages 2 and 3 were likewise obliterated and all that was left of page 4 was 'Your devoted husband, Tom'. At least an explanatory note was enclosed by the censor, to the effect that, 'Madame, your husband is quite well but is much too communicative'.

Special green envelopes were issued for letters of a 'very private nature' and these were not censored within the battalion. They were stamped and certified: 'I certify that the contents refer to nothing but private and family matters.' However, further checks were carried out at Base HQ, and if a letter in a green envelope was found to contain additional, non-private material, the whole company in question could be deprived of green envelopes for a period.

Alfred Burrage found a way to skirt round censorship in Bavincourt in 1917. Actually, he had been trying to chat up a friendly padre and was on the point of sealing an arrangement with him to send uncensored letters, when Burrage was observed by the padre playfully wrestling with a girl outside an *estaminet*. As a character reference this was a disaster: he thought it would only make matters worse if he tried to explain that it really was wrestling they were doing. Luckily, all was not lost, because Burrage then met an Army Service Corps driver who had stacks of green envelopes for sale (ASC drivers were possibly the forerunners of the spiv). For 2 francs Burrage obtained a pile of green envelopes which would last him for years.

Classic Letters

Some letters stand out as classics. R.E. Vernède copied out an example from one of his platoon – 'a nice boy', who wrote home every single night with the identical message:

> Dear Mum and Dad and dear loving sisters Rosie, Letty and our Gladys. I am very pleased to write you another welcome letter as this leaves me. Dear Mum and Dad and loving sisters, I hopes you keeps the home fires burning. Not arf. The boys are in the pink. Not arf. Dear loving sisters Rosie, Letty and our Gladys, keep merry and bright. Not arf ...

" Never mind, 'Erb, perhaps there's a postcard in it for you ! "

Published by kind permission of the family of Bert Thomas.

The letter continued in this vein for three pages and he never changed a word – every night. If he wanted to give them some real news he wrote a separate letter. But there was always this daily expression of familial love. You don't know whether to laugh or cry.

A letter written in Foncquevillers on 27 September 1915 ended: 'God bless you and keep you from your loving cousin Tom.'

'Dear Brother', began another one, 'I can't tell you where I am but I am at the place which I left to go to the place where I've come from.' (This could fool any spy.)

'Dere [sic] wife. If you could make the next postal order a trifle stronger I might be getting an egg to my tea, Your loving husband, Jas. Muckleware, No. 74077.'

More Sex in the Letters

Captain R. McDonald (7/Queen's Own Cameron Highlanders) was eagerly awaiting his leave and particularly his wife, Jeannie: 'I am expecting leave soon. Take a good look at the floor. You'll see nothing but the ceiling when I get home.'

'Yours retro-spectively' was how one girl signed off to a Tommy, after giving him the elbow in favour of the local milkman. Lieutenant Crerar was doing his nightly read of his men's letters when he came across a missive which concluded: '... your loving husband, Joe. P.S. I wunner who yer sleeping with tonight ye auld bitch.'

Private 'Cosh' (that's how he signed his letters) exhibited a 'wooden exterior' according to his platoon commander, but he was conducting four love affairs simultaneously. They were far-flung, possibly indicating previous postings: Coatbridge (Scotland), South Kensington, Kelvinside and Hampshire. He became extremely annoyed with the one in South Kensington in early 1915 because she also announced she was going out with the milkman – in fact, she was engaged to be married to him.

Of course, love letters travelled in both directions and it is dreadful to contemplate the ultimate fate of some of the outward-bound ones – heartfelt and steamy outpourings. The grave shortage of toilet paper spelt a certain end to them – especially those of the 'Dear John' variety and especially if Tommy was making way for the milkman. Andrew Bowie (1/Cameron Highlanders) observed that love letters had to be particularly spicy to escape the latrine.

One cannot guess the fate of a letter sent by one of Robert Graves' company, a clever admission of some hanky-panky in the rest areas eased by a profession of true love: 'French girls are nice to sleep with but not as good as you, my wife. I miss you very much.'

Myriads of letters were marked 'S.W.A.K.' ('sealed with a kiss') on the flap of the envelope, but in fact it was the company commander who sealed them.

Complaints

Some letters were business letters. Major Desmond Young, 1/15 Londons (Civil Service Rifles), who was responsible for the officers' mess of the battalion, wrote to complain about some whisky recently purchased from a firm in Scotland (October 1918). He must have gone over the top in his condemnation of this '9th Hole Whisky' because the firm wrote back complaining about the tone of Young's letter. They were of the view that some of his comments about their 9th Hole Whisky were uncalled for, if not downright offensive. However, they concluded in a more conciliatory vein, they would include Young's letter in their album of curiosities of the war. Undeterred, Young wrote again: 'Dear Sir, I advise you also to include in your collection of curiosities of the war a bottle of your 9th Hole Whisky.'

A to Z of Words

A BLOODY BALLS-UP: A general reply to any request for information regarding military progress, e.g. as uttered by a wounded man of the Middlesex Regiment in response to Dick Richards' polite enquiry about how the Battle of Loos was going (26 September 1915).
ADJECTIVAL AND BORING: An opinion of the obscene language of the Londoners of the 8/Royal Fusiliers expressed by an Australian soldier.

ALLIGATOR: Private Cecil Withers of the 7/East Surreys recalled an incident when a comrade was hauled up before his CO for having dirty boots, dirty buttons and long hair. Lieutenant-Colonel: 'Who's brought these allegations?' CSM: 'Sir, I am the alligator.'

ALL OLD CROCKS: Army Ordnance Corps.

ARE WE DOWNHEARTED?: The 2/Grenadier Guards were arriving at Le Havre on 18 August 1914 and were greeted warmly by French troops. In keeping with the upbeat mood, a lone Tommy called from the forecastle: 'Are we downhearted?' This generated a massive response from the crowded ship: 'No, we're not!'

You can't put a precise date on the transformation but the normal answer to this question later in the war changed to, 'Yes, we are!' It was possibly during the Battle of the Somme, maybe earlier, certainly not later. It is one way of looking at the history of the war. Anyway, if some brave souls were still inclined to respond with a patriotic 'No', some other smart arse would add: 'Then you damn well soon will be!'

ARMY ROCKS: Socks. Private Bernard Livermore (2/20 Londons – the 'Long 'Un' you met in the opening chapter) received a pair of socks from an auntie. They reached up to his bum and were quickly christened 'Toulouse' and 'Toulon'. Auntie had over-estimated even Bernard's considerable length.

BACKS TO THE WALL: A special order was issued by Sir Douglas Haig on Thursday 11 April 1918, during the great German offensive: 'With our backs to the wall and believing in the justice of our cause, each of us must fight to the end.' More than one Tommy was overheard asking: 'What f***ing wall?'

BALLOONATICS: Observers who went up in large balloons to trace enemy positions and movements. It was a very dangerous occupation.

BALOO: Bailleul.

BANDAGHEM: Nickname of a hospital in Flanders using the common Flemish suffix 'ghem'. There was also 'Dosinghem' and 'Mendinghem'.

BEEF HEARTS: Army beans – rhyming slang alluding to the effects of the beans.

BERKELEY HUNT: Another piece of rhyming slang used when you wanted to call someone a fool. The phrase was also often shortened to 'berk'.

BOMBARDIER FRITZ: *Pommes de terre frites* – chips.

BY THE TESTIMONIALS: An alternative version of 'by the short and curlies'.

CHAPLAIN: From the trench magazine of the Royal Naval Division – *Mudhook* – a poem from a padre:

A French 'language' lesson.

I do not wish to hurt you
But (Bang!) I feel I must.
It is a Christian virtue
To lay you in the dust.
You (Zip! That bullet got you).
You're really better dead.
I'm sorry that I shot you.
Here, let me hold your head.

COLLEGE: This was the soubriquet given to the 39 General Hospital, which specialised in treating venereal diseases. A soldier who went through the full treatment here was said to have 'graduated'.

COMIC CUTS: Second Lieutenant C.M. Slack of the 4/East Yorkshires referred to the *Daily Brigade Trench Paper* as 'comic cuts' (22 January 1916), indicating that all the worst news was omitted.

COOKHOUSE OFFICIAL: A rumour – often about the next destination of a battalion and usually wildly inaccurate.

COOK'S TOURIST: Visitors to the trenches – very brief and on quiet fronts.

CUTHBERT: An officer in a cushy job well behind the front line.

DAILY PREVARICATOR: This was the nickname given to the *Daily Mail*. The editions printed in Britain tended to paint a rosy picture of the war – 'our brave lads' and 'victory is imminent' – Horatio Bottomley stuff. In fairness to the journal, anything different was mutilated by the censors. They were less successful with continental editions, more likely to be read by those who could see what was happening.

DI-AGONISE: Due to the pressures put on the medical services by the Spanish flu epidemic of 1918, some quite junior RAMC orderlies found themselves in very responsible positions. One isolation hospital was run by an ex-stretcher-bearer (or 'body-snatcher'). An invalid observed: 'Fancy putting a young feller like that in charge. As if he could di-agonise.'

EAT APPLES: Étaples.

EAT LESS AND SAVE SHIPPING: Due to the severe food shortages in Britain by February 1918, there was support for the idea of reducing the amount given to the troops on the Western Front. The CSM of the 13/Royal Fusiliers put up a notice reading: 'Eat less and save shipping.' But someone altered it to read: 'Eat less and save shitting.'

Graffiti was commonly added to official notices in this way, e.g. the transport officer at High Wood (Somme) in 1917 efficiently put up a rail timetable, but it was continually adorned with additions such as: 'Who says?' – 'I don't think so' – 'It never come yesterday'.

EH! MOSSOO!: This was how a British sergeant addressed a Portuguese NCO, as in, '*Eh! Mossoo! Nous patrolio tonighto. Compri?*' To which his ally replied diplomatically, '*Oui, monsieur*' (reported by Major R.T. Rees).

EMBELLISHMENT: One Tommy found it extremely difficult to work with another man, whom, he pointed out, 'had been done for embellishment'.

FLYING ARSEHOLES: This referred to an RFC officer's badge – an 'O' with a wing.

FLYING COMMODE: Sidney Rogerson's description of a certain type of German mine. This raised a hearty guffaw from his men. It made him realise, according to him, how easy it was to make them laugh.

FRIGIFIED: Frozen feet.

GOGGLE-EYED BOOGER WITH A TIT: This was the common description of the gas helmet issued in March 1916. Robert Graves was unable to wear it properly because of a crooked nose, the result of a rugby accident, followed by a boxing accident. He had it fixed in London in April 1916 and thereafter wore the 'booger' successfully.

HAVE NOTHING TO DO WITH THE DIARRHOEA EXCUSE: Advice to officers in a pamphlet about men disrupting marches (March 1917).

The 'Goggle-eyed booger with a tit'.

I CAN'T STAND NO MORE OF THIS MAC – BLOODY – F***ING – ONOCHIE: The use of internal modifiers to emphasise one's point.

INSINUATOR: In early March 1916 Lieutenant Eberle, at Henn, near Doullens, told off one of his cooks for leaving lots of empty food tins around. 'Well, sir,' explained the cook, 'it's as 'ow they're building an insinuator and I was going to put 'em in it.'

JIPPO: Meat fat.

JUST-A-MINUTE: An *estaminet*.

MURPHYISED: Asleep. A double distortion of 'the arms of Morpheus' into 'the arms of Murphy' and 'murphyised', e.g. 'No, I didn't see it, I was murphyised.'

NAPOO: From the French '*Il n'y en a plus*'. Used precisely, it meant 'there is no more', but it was broadened into a wide range of meanings: I have none; you have none; there are none; finished; no good; there never was any; I am no more; I am destroyed; no good.

Used as a dispirited general view of the war, and one's own poor prospects, it indicated disapproval, disenchantment, obliteration, etc.

NICKY: A fag end – just enough for two draws and a fit of coughing.

NOTICES: It was a bit like roads today – notices everywhere – official and unofficial: 'Troops are forbidden to bomb fish. By order of the Town Major' (spotted by Robert Graves by the canal in Béthune); 'The French authorities intend to preserve this village untouched as a relic of the war. It is strictly forbidden to remove anything or otherwise alter its appearance' (Gommecourt, March 1918, put up shortly before intense German shelling rearranged it completely); 'If you are in the habit of spitting on the carpet at home, please spit here. Receptacle provided' (in Talbot House, Poperinghe).

Indented in the chalk wall of a trench with a jackknife, and coloured in purple pencil (22 May 1915), was: 'I have no pain, dear Mother, now, but lummy I do feel dry, so fix me to a brewery and leave me there to die.' (This was seen by Captain Rowland Feilding of the 3/Coldstream Guards; they were actually the words of a song sung to the tune of *My Love is Like a Red, Red Rose*, which was also the marching song of the Loyal North Lancasters.)

'Paradise Lost' – a name plate pinned up by sappers of the 2nd Field Company, Royal Engineers, over a pig sty during warm weather near 'Plugstreet' Wood in May 1915.

'Bomb-throwing Competition – Dummies Only Please' (a reassuring notice about an event at the 110 Infantry Brigade's Tournament at Moyenville, 16 August 1917).

Near Ypres on 17 September 1917, in very bad weather:

> The world wasn't built in a day
> And Eve didn't ride in a bus.
> But most of the world is in a sandbag
> And the rest of it's plastered on us.

Hung over a bridge of the River Yser, which was registered by German artillery: 'You may loiter on this bridge: it inspires confidence.' A notice was also displayed, near Arras in April 1917, in a notoriously dangerous area. 'For f***'s sake don't f*** around here, signed, D. Haig.' It was removed and then reappeared again, probably by popular request. Prime suspects were the New Zealand tunnellers.

NYD: A medical term meaning 'Not Yet Diagnosed' but often interpreted (especially by the patient) as 'Not Yet Dead'.

OFFICERS ONLY: Old Orkney whisky – very good.

POPULAR SAYINGS: It is very unlucky to be killed on a Friday; if the sun rises in the east there will be soup for lunch; if bread is the staff of life what is the life of staff? Answer – a loaf.

PROPERTY OWNER: Corpse.

RAGOUT MACONOCHIE: Open one tin of Maconochie Ration. Warm gently until the greasy oil floats on the top. Remove this by blotting up with a piece of four by two flannelette. Place this on one side for later use. Remove the black lumps in the Mc Ration. These are potatoes. Squeeze out the greasy oil from the four by two into a frying pan and gently fry the potatoes. Take two handfuls of dry vegetables. (They look very much like any other dried leaves.) Mix with a little water flavoured with chloride of lime and pat into croutons. These should be gently fried after the potatoes are cooked. Re-heat the Mc Ration and serve the whole on cold enamel plates.

ROOTY GONG: A popular name for a long-service medal, which was widely recognised as a reward for eating army rations for eighteen years and for undetected crime over the same period.

SAN FAIRY ANN: Distorted from the French *'ça ne fait rien'* – it doesn't matter; it makes no difference, why worry? The phrase was extremely popular with the troops because of its inherent cynicism, fatalism – a shrugging of the shoulders – whatever.

SCENE-SHIFTER: The name given to an enormous field gun near Arras in 1917.

SIXTY-POUNDER: Suet pudding.

SPUD HOLE: Guardroom.

STAR OF THE MOVIES: Number Nine pill for constipation.

TALKING RUPERT: Mimicking posh officers. Some Tommies were very good at it; some of them actually spoke like that.

TANKS: Each tank had a name and additional ones were given by infantry as they trundled by, e.g. at Cambrai on 20 November 1917, the first big tank offensive: 'Here's an old bitch!'; 'There goes a great f***ing bull!'; 'Look at that skidding, weaving barstard!'; 'What a whopper!'; 'Go on, Charlie boy, flatten f***ing Fritz!'

Official names included Dracula, Fairy, Fiara, Foam and Old Mother Hubbard. Gravedigger appeared earlier at Pilckem Ridge (Ypres) on 31

A tank and its messenger. Reproduced by kind permission of the Imperial War Museum (Q9247).

July 1917; instead of the more usual 6-pounder guns it was festooned with machine guns.

THREE BITCHES: Tommy's name for one brand of army-issue fags – 'Three Witches'. They tasted like seaweed, according to Alfred Burrage. Older soldiers were used to these foul cigarettes. Sergeant Bill Partridge (7/Middlesex) had, in fact, smoked them since he was 11, and also "Arf a Mo' (see earlier illustration), 'Ruby Queen' and 'Ruby Hussar'. At the age of 93 he was warned by his GP that smoking at the rate he did was bad for him.

TRENCH PUDDING: Take four hardtack biscuits. Place in dishcloth and bang with entrenching tool handle until pulverised. Soak in water for two to three hours, until it is a pulpy mess. Add one tin of Tommy Tickler's plum and apple jam. Stir well. Heat over a

" Give us a fag and I'll give yer an 'orse."

Published by kind permission of the family of Bert Thomas.

brisk fire and when the bottom burns serve with a teaspoon per person of condensed milk. This should be more than enough for four persons.

ZIG-ZAG: Overheard in a shop: '*Marie, ally promenade ce soir?*' suggested a Tommy. '*Non, pas ce soir*,' Marie turns him down. '*Moi, ally au estaminet, revenir zig-zag si vous no promenade*' (i.e. if you don't come out with me I'll get sozzled).

Favourite Songs

The soldiers loved a good old sing-song to keep up their spirits when on long marches, in billets and in *estaminets*. Imagine the joy to be had after getting well-oiled to blast out familiar ditties with all your mates, hopefully with someone on the joanna (piano). Even those who were too skint to drink could get merry on the fumes and the general bonhomie.

> Oh, you beautiful doll,
> You great big, beautiful doll.
> Let me put my arms around you,
> I could never live without you ...

Here we are Again was another popular and innocent refrain, especially apt at certain times. A battalion marching after sixteen days at the front line, near Arras in April 1917, weary, dirty, hungry and soaked to the skin, finally reached its designated billets. But then a captain said there had been a mistake and they had to march two more hours to the proper resting place. They trudged off again, too dispirited to sing. After two hours they arrived at the billet and it was exactly the one they had left two hours previously. This time they burst into spontaneous song:

> Here we are again,
> Happy as can be,
> All good pals
> And jolly good company.

SUNG AROUND LT. DOBBIE'S GRAMOPHONE
IN HIS BILLET— ESQUELBECQ, NORD.
MID AUGUST 1918.

"At One and Two - I'm with Maud and Lou;
Three and Four - two girls more.
At Five and Six with some dears I fix
Seven - Eight Clara and Caroline.
Nine and Ten - I'm at work again;
Eleven it's Kate - Gee she's Great!
But the Girl I meet at Twelve —
Oh I say - What a Life!
Not a word to the Wife!
Tick Tock winds up the clock
And I'll start the day over again"

"Another little drink, another little drink,
Another little drink wouldn't
do us any harm."

"When one has one,
One wants one little one more.
One has one, one has two —
One has three or four!
What did Gladstone say in 84- ? - Why-
"When one has one little one —
One wants one little one more!"

"Tell me LILAC DOMINO,
Where does your garden grow?
All eyes seem to follow you
As you flutter to and fro
And like a Butterfly
Flutter by and go!
But where you go
I must follow
LILAC. LILAC DOMINO!"

"Kitty, Kitty - Isn't it a pity
In The City you work so hard
With your One. Two, Three and Four
And Six, Seven Eight GERRARD
Kitty, Kitty, Isn't it a pity
That you're wasting so much Time,
With your lips glued to the Telephone
When they might be close to mine!"

"Hello — c'est vous?"
"Oui - c'est moi - ça va-t-il?"
"Non car vous tenez mon cœur par un fil"
"Oh dites moi, je le veux —
Le couleur de vos cheveux
Mais ils sont blonds, si vous les aimex blonds
Aimez les vous noirs ils sont de noir profond
Mieux pas s'aimer sans jamais se contacter
Qui sait? Peutêtre C'est la meilleure façon."

"CLICQUOT - CLICQUOT!
Wine of London Town!
Old London, where the lights are-
Where the sights are, where the nights are
In the Amber of your Bubbles
Is the Sea to drown all troubles.
From London Bridge to Earls Court
I'll never Homeward bound
God Bless you damn you CLICQUOT
You make the World go round!"

"Any old night is a wonderful night
If you're out with a wonderful girl!
If you're out with and music and dancing
Dining and dancing in a whirl.
All set the old heart in a whirl.
All set the high nights - the dry nights I'll never forget - for
I like the high nights some nights I'll never forget - for
But those nights is a wonderful night!
Any old night is a wonderful girl!"
If you're out with a wonderful girl!"

"We'd have a little cottage
In a little Town
We'd have a little Mistress
In a little Gown.
A little Garden, a little Cat.
A little Doorstep, with WELCOME on the Mat.
We'd have a little trouble and we'd have a little Strike
But all these things will happen
when you've got a little Wife!
We should be as happy as the Angels up above
With our little Cottage and a lot of LOVE!"

Read. 70.

Drawing by I.L. Read.

"STAND TO"

DECEMBER EVENING 1915. MONCHY MILL - 97 TRENCH
'COCKNEY'NEWMAN conducting Salvationist service thus:-
"Nah that Sister Mary there 'as testified (several 'Allelujahs!)
we'll all sing together number Two Twoty Two in the Red Book -
JOYFUL WILL THE MEETING BE!' • • • Then ••
     "ANOTHER SHILLING ON THE DRUM BROTHERS!"· · · ·
·· followed by distinct sounds of laughter from the German
   73rd. Fusilier Regiment of Hanover - (25/30 yds. away in the
Trench opposite) , and two quick bullets into our parapet.

Drawing by I.L. Read.

Settled into a favourite *estaminet* the songs could take a different direction. The following was sung to the tune of *Mademoiselle from Armentières, parlez-vous* and with the words of *The Landlady's Daughter*, written by the German poet J.L. Uhland:

A German officer crossed the Rhine, skibboo! Skibboo!
A German officer crossed the Rhine.
He was on the look-out for women and wine, skibboo! Skibboo!
Ski-bumpity-bump skibboo!

Oh, landlord, have you a daughter fair? Skibboo! Skibboo!
Oh, landlord have you a daughter fair,
With lily-white breasts and golden hair, skibboo!?
Ski-bumpity-bump skibboo!

(Last verse)
It's a hell of a song that we've just sung, skibboo!
It's a hell of a song that we've just sung
And the fellow that wrote it ought to be hung, skibboo! Skibboo!
Ski-bumpity-bump skibboo!

Dirty Ditties & Recitations

There was also a staple diet of ribald songs. This was one sung by Arthur Shoeing Smith of the 5/Oxon and Bucks Light Infantry at a Christmas dinner in 1916 near Albert. It was called the 'Apple Song':

I knew a fellow, his name was Ben.
He had nine of a family (nearly ten!) ...
Now, all you gents, if you want any more
I've an apple up me arse
And you can have the core.

The lieutenant-colonel called Arthur over and he thought he was in trouble, but in fact the CO wanted more of the same. Arthur went through his complete repertoire of scurrilous songs as he gulped down as much champagne and beer as the officers could supply. They kindly carried him back to his billet.

Possibly officers of the 94 Field Ambulance, at their rest station at Couin on the same day, also made use of the Shoeing Smith album. A drunk captain rendered: 'I've a hole in an elephant's bottom.' Unfortunately, it was against army regulations to sing a song of this nature and fighting broke out amongst drunken officers.

Other songs relied on innuendo:

> There was a gay Cavallero
> Who dwelt on the banks of the Navaro,
> Flashing about with his wonderful,
> Wonderful to-ra-la, to-ra-li-ay!

This was a favourite of the 2/Queen's, whose standard marching song as they approached destinations was, 'Here they come, here they come, bloody great barstards every one.'

A large number of dirty songs featured emasculation – perhaps the Tommies felt emasculated stuck out in this wilderness.

> The Squire had a daughter, so fair and so tall.
> She lived in her satins and silks at the hall.
> But she married a man with no balls at all,
> No balls at all,
> No balls at all,
> She married a man with no balls at all.

This condition also featured in countless jokes which went the rounds of the Western Front. If you had not heard them all after a few months out there you weren't getting out enough, e.g. 'The wild man of Borneo had no balls. That's why he was so wild' (boom! boom!). To give you an idea of the stature of these popular jokes, another favourite was about the Cockney who stood outside a dugout in a captured German trench. He called out, 'Anybody there?'

'Nein,' came a voice from the interior.

'Nine, eh? Well, bloody well share this amongst yer' (throwing down a Mills bomb).

> It was Christmas Day in the harem
> And the eunuchs were standing around.
> In strode the bold, bad Sultan
> And gazed at his marble halls.
> 'What would you like for Christmas, boys?'
> And the eunuchs answered, 'Balls!'
> [This was delivered like rap.]

Unpopular Sergeants

Many songs were anti-sergeant. The great bulk of sergeants were smashing blokes, very popular with the men, but there must have been a few who weren't, otherwise these songs would not have been sung, including the infamous *Never Mind*:

> If the Sergeant pinched your rum swearing blind.
> If the Sergeant's pinched your rum, never mind.
> He's entitled to a tot
> But he drunk the bloomin' lot.
> If the Sergeant pinched your rum, never mind.

Smiler Marshall sang his version of this with great gusto in 2001 for a BBC documentary:

> If the Sergeant's pinched your rum, never mind, never mind.
> If the Sergeant's pinched your rum, just swear and blind.
> They're entitled to a tot, but they drink the bloody lot.
> If the Sergeant pinched your rum, just never mind.

Actually, the original *Never Mind* was sung during the Christmas truce of 1914:

If old Jerry shells the trench,
Never mind!
Though the blasted sandbags fly
You only have once to die.
If old Jerry shells the trench,
Never mind!
If you get stuck on the wire,
Never mind!
If you get stuck on the wire,
Never mind!

Sergeant-majors were also fair game:

We've got a Sergeant-Major
Who's never seen a gun.
He's mentioned in dispatches
For drinking Private's rum.
And when he sees old Jerry
You should see the bugger run
Miles and miles behind the line.

(CSMs and RSMs usually joined in this jolly marching song.)

Rear Admirals

Much was composed about the brave men who ran the trench latrines
– 'rear admirals'.

Dan, Dan, the sanitary man.
Working underground all day
Sweeping up urinals
Picking up the finals
Whiling the hours away –
Gor Blimey!

> Doing his little bit
> Shovelling up the shit
> He's so blithe and gay
> And the only music he hears
> Is poo-poo-poo-poo-poo all day.

('Finals' were final editions of newspapers or football results from evening papers.)

The tune of *Colonel Bogy* was used for a lot of songs, including one for the rear admirals:

> We are the night shit-shifters,
> We shift the shite at night.

'Mutiny'

Indeed, well-known tunes and hymns were frequently adapted, rather in the way football supporters use them these days for their favourite chants. Sang to the tune of *Oh, God, our Help in Ages Past* (e.g. by the 2/RWF in March 1915 in billets near Bois Grenier):

> John Wesley had a little dog.
> He was so very thin.
> He took him to the Gates of Hell
> And threw the bastard in.

You can see how inconsequential so many of these songs and recitations were; it was in keeping with the philosophy of – San Fairy Anne – who cares? It was about the nearest Tommy came to mutiny. Blasphemy particularly inspired him, along with anything hinting at working-class rebellion:

> It was Christmas Day in the workhouse,
> That season of good cheer.
> The paupers' hearts were merry,
> Their bellies full of beer.

> The pompous workhouse master,
> As he strode about the halls,
> Wished them a Merry Christmas,
> But the paupers answered 'Balls!'
>
> This angered the workhouse master
> Who swore by all the gods
> That he'd stop their Christmas pudden,
> The dirty rotten sods.
> Then up spake a bald-headed pauper,
> His face as bold as brass,
> 'You can keep your Christmas pudden
> And stick it up your arse.'

Allied to this 'mutiny' was the feeling of helplessness. *We're Here, Because We're Here, Because We're Here* was sung to the tune of *Auld Lang Syne* when the Tommies didn't have a bloody clue where they were (e.g. the 7/Royal Warwickshires in August 1915 – they were actually taking over ex-French trenches at Hébuterne).

I Want to Be at Home

This theme was often featured in marching songs:

> I don't want to be a soldier
> I don't want to go to war.
> I'd rather stay at home
> Around the streets to roam.
> And live on the earnings of a well-paid whore.
>
> Far, far from Ypres I long to be
> Where German snipers cannot shoot at me.
> Deep in my dugout, where the worms creep
> Waiting for the Sergeant to kiss me to sleep.

> I don't want a bayonet up my arse-hole,
> I don't want my bollocks shot away.
> I'd rather stay in England
> And f*** my bloody life away.

(The above was sung to the air *On Sunday I Walk Out with a Soldier* from *The Passing Show*, a revue at the London Hippodrome, 1914.)

> Why did we join the Army, boys?
> Why did we join the Army?
> Why did we come to France to fight?
> We must have been bloody-well barmy.

Self-Deprecation

At the end of the day, Tommy could be self-deprecating, perhaps in the most famous song of all, *We are Fred Karno's Army*, sung to *The Church's One Foundation*. Fred Karno was a popular music-hall comedian who eventually ran a company of fellow comedians, including Charlie Chaplin (until he went to Hollywood for fame and fortune). Fred's taste for comedy was inclined to the absurd.

> We are Fred Karno's Army,
> The ragtime infantry.
> We cannot fight, we cannot shoot,
> What bloody use are we?
> And when we get to Berlin,
> The Kaiser he vill say,
> Hoch! Hoch! Mein Gott!
> What a bloody fine lot
> Are the ragtime infantry!

Anyway, they were better than the Jerries – they did get to Berlin. There was no defeatism here, just a belief in general cock-ups and incompetence leading to final victory. It was quite a prophecy.

ELEVEN

Who Ate All the Pigeons?

Plunder

The Wipers Times (12 February 1916) hinted that some carrier pigeons had gone missing. Who had appropriated them? Was it a 'brunette' infantry officer? Was it he who had prepared a special dinner of pigeon for some special guests? And who were they?

There was further plunder at the Expeditionary Force Canteen in Bapaume in March 1918. Jerry was at the gates of the town and, in order to save thousands of pounds worth of stock from falling into the hands of the enemy, British and colonial troops were forced to eat, drink and smoke it. 377 Battery gunners prepared to fire at Fritz with long Pantellos in their mouths and bottles of Bass beer in their hands. Passing officers were offered a choice of whisky, gin, beer, stout, champagne, wincarnis, port, Benedictine, crème de menthe or lime juice.

In the EFC, marquee men were climbing over the counters and pulling down stacks of tins and boxes. An EFC attendant commented to a 377 officer: 'There's no objectshen at all to all the lads helping themselves, because far better they get it than the 'uns, but pleash purra guard over the whisky or theesh chaps won't be 'alf blind.'

The CSM had a case of tins of café au lait, nine large tins of biscuits and five pounds of tobacco. The adjutant had 700 cigarettes, six dozen Gillette razor blades, one Ingersoll watch, one patent combined tin-opener and corkscrew, one whole roast chicken, two bottles of Grand Marnier and 144 boxes of Beecham's Pills (worth £151 4s).

Enterprise

Military enterprise prevailed throughout the war. A crack shot of the 2/Grenadier Guards shot seven Jerries in woods near Ypres on 8 November 1914 and four pheasants. Lieutenant Carr of 377 Battery, Royal Artillery, filed a special report on a daring night raid on the enemy on 4 May 1916. The 'enemy' in this case was the bees whose hives the engineers plundered so bravely. There were casualties, but a return of two dixies of honey was sweet success. All was planned by the enterprising battery CO, Major Sutherland.

Enterprise was easier when it fell off the back of lorries (or GS wagons), as in the case of some merry men of the 17/Leicesters returning from a night out in an *estaminet* in April 1917. A carcass of mutton fell off a wagon and landed at their feet. Desperately they tried to attract the attention of the driver, but to no avail, and they were forced to carry the mutton back to their cookhouse and reluctantly get the cooks to cook it, at the cost of a few Woodbines.

The 2/West Yorkshires were busy fighting the Battle of the Aisne in September 1914 but took time off to procure some chickens from a farm. The farmer's wife complained bitterly about this outrage to Captain James Jack. She also confirmed that every one of the stolen chickens was a layer of the first order – indeed, champions. Jack went round his company with a hat and 'suggested' that every man put something in it. The farmer's wife was hoping that the rest of her chickens would disappear in the same way at the price she got for those which had already vanished.

Lieutenant-Colonel Osburn, CO of the 14 Corps Field Ambulance (July 1915), had to negotiate in a similar way with a Flemish farmer near Poperinghe. Private Brown was accused of stealing an egg from him. But Brown made out a strong defence, of which even Fizzer Green of the 2/RWF would have been proud. Brown informed Lieutenant-Colonel Osburn that there had been a hole in a fence and that he had stuck his hand in it as an act of sheer curiosity. Amazingly, his hand came to rest on a newly laid egg; it was still warm. He removed this egg, said Brown, in order to ensure that it got to the farmer whilst still warm and fresh. The CO was still anxious to know why Brown was running away from the farmer when the latter overtook him. Private Brown was of the opinion that he was getting the egg back to the farm in the shortest possible time and he hadn't been too sure if the farmer, who was old, could run faster than he. Moreover, this citizen of Flanders had been unpleasant. 'He said some 'orrible things to me, sir,' declared Private Brown. 'I think he's a German spy, sir.'

A baker's wife was just as heroic in the defence of her product. She was in a small bake house in Arras in April 1917 when Private Carson Stewart (6/Cameron Highlanders) entered. However, with the Battle of Arras raging outside, shells started falling in the road and she wisely fled to the basement. Stewart took this opportunity to remove 'du pang' off a shelf but Madame, who suspected that something like this would happen, made a sudden dash aloft and caught him red-handed. She chased him from the premises screaming, 'Brigand! Brigand!' It was not surprising, then, that the *patronne* at a billet in Laventie (10 November 1915) was so pleased with '*les soldats*' of the 4/Coldstream Guards. They had stolen no chickens at all, and only a few eggs, during their sojourn with her. It was a record.

It worked both ways: Sergeant Beechey of the 2/Lincolns was asked to pay 3 francs for a tin of peaches. 'Who do you think I am?' he demanded of the opportunistic shopkeeper. 'Rothschild? Carnegie? No bon, no bon! Finis!' Such negotiations resulted in the development of much 'franglais'. But Private Bobett preferred sign language: for eggs he squatted down, flapped imaginary wings and squawked, which just goes to show that not all Tommies were rude.

There were other types of enterprise: the wily old soldiers of the 2/RWF were out in Béthune in April 1915 flogging army jam to the natives at 4 francs a tin (exorbitant). At least, at that time, the tins really contained jam, albeit plum and apple jam. A year later they were still hawking the stuff around but the tins contained foot grease. They sold it on the day before they were due back on the front line, hoping by the time they returned to the town (if they did) the people would have forgotten or forgiven. As the 'Old Soldier' observed, it was very good quality foot grease.

Equally misleading was the claim by a staff officer that the Yser Canal (late in 1915) was famous for its oysters. The waterway, having endured two major battles, was a sluggish, stinking mess with the occasional corpse floating to the surface. He made his assertion to a merry band of Brigade HQ staff, out for the day. But fellow staff officers challenged their comrade to actually prove there were oysters around by doing a spot of fishing. The wily captain sought to wriggle out of this difficult situation by pointing out that there was no suitable bait available. Fishing for oysters required very special bait.

All was not lost, however, because the brigade intelligence officer was present and he knew for a fact that pieces of padre were very succulent as far as oysters were concerned. Sitting on the bank, enjoying a bit of sunny weather, there was a padre. The intelligence officer averred that the padre could be put to very good use by cutting him up into little pieces and feeding him to the oysters. They approached the good man and put forward their plan – no offence intended. Curiously, the padre must have been a member of that odd community – those with no sense of humour. He edged uneasily away, also asserting that he felt sure the canal was in such a mess that oysters couldn't possibly survive in there. There was a brief flirtation with the idea of throwing him in the canal whole, but better sense prevailed.

Hunting

Major Poore, the CO of the 2/RWF, was invited on a wild boar hunt by local French nobility. It was a most enjoyable day in the woods near Albert. The major bagged a rabbit and a squirrel. The rabbit was handed to him in a brown paper parcel.

Captain G.R. Cassels of the 176 Tunnelling Company, returning from leave, brought with him grouse from the Yorkshire Moors. Sadly, there were serious delays in the Channel due to submarine activity (July 1916) and it took several days for Cassels and the grouse to arrive back at camp. By this time the birds were a seething mass of maggots. But nothing could beat army cooks, or, in this case, batmen. Private Hart beautifully cooked the grouse and added a delicious white sauce.

Cassels and his guests came round and personally congratulated Hart on his achievement. Little did they know that the white sauce was made from the maggots.

More Flavour

Tins of pork and beans formed a solid part of army rations but their quality varied. Indeed, sometimes Tommy was hard put to find any pork at all, despite extensive searches. Lieutenant Tyndale-Biscoe complained to Brigade HQ. Brigade replied that troops should not be disappointed if there appeared to be no pork in the tins of pork and beans. What commonly happened, they pointed out, was that the meat could become absorbed into the beans. Tyndale-Biscoe was not to be fobbed off so lightly, so sent another stiff note asserting that, in that case, the whole ration of meat could be delivered in 'meat lozenges'.

But there was no mistaking the presence of HP ('Houses of Parliament') sauce on 7 June 1917 in a communication trench coming up the front line below Messines Ridge. This was a fateful day because the top of the ridge, in German hands, had been blown up by a million tons of TNT taken along in tunnels under enemy lines. This most successful day was made even more spicy due to the fact that one soldier had dropped and smashed his precious bottle of HP sauce. The delicious aroma filled the trench as men filed by, enriching their day. Everyone was cheered by it, except the poor bloke who had dropped it.

The digestive juices of Winston Groom and his machine gun team were equally stimulated in an idyllic orchard near Arras in April 1917. This month had started off with snow but now they had a nice evening to sit under the trees and look forward to the chicken being cooked by the farmer's wife. They were almost drifting off to sleep, fortified by some *vin blanc*, when she hurried out accompanied by a delicious aroma. Winston Groom stood up, carving knife at the ready, and then his face fell. The chicken's head was still attached to the rest of it. He poked around and discovered that its innards were still inside too. Perhaps the horrible truth was that Madame had never cooked a chicken before; or perhaps they ate chicken like this, not wasting any of it.

Winston stuck the knife in it and held it aloft, singing the soldiers' chorus from *Faust*. The chicken had not had a good life: it was all bones and great lumps of fat. One of the other machine-gunners suggested it had perished during the Crimean War. Madame could see they weren't happy with it. 'No bon?' she enquired sadly.

'No bon,' confirmed Winston, just as sadly.

But all's well that ends well. The lovely evening was saved by some fat pork, which was to have been the farmer's dinner. What he had instead Winston did not record; perhaps he ate the chicken. Maybe he liked chicken like this. Anyway, the soldiers enjoyed the pork and it was really a splendid evening, with the sun glinting through the trees. The farmer's wife piled on the *vin blanc*. They were happy soldiers after all.

Fish

Millions of parcels were sent from home to the troops on the Western Front during the war. Very sadly, some of them did not reach the men they were intended for owing to the war (and not the British Forces Post Office, who did a marvellous job). There was nothing for it but to share the contents amongst those who had survived. Rifleman Stanley Hopkins was handed a tin of dark 'jam'. He stuck his spoon in it and ladled out a mouthful, which he promptly spat out. ''Ere,' he complained loudly, 'this pozzy tastes of fish.' (It was caviar, which had not featured in Stanley's diet before.)

But fish was definitely on the menu (or intended menu) for some soldiers. After recovering from Spanish flu in May 1918, George Weeks did a spot of fishing in the River Ancre at Avuluy, with a stick for a rod and a nail with a worm on the end of it. He didn't catch a thing. But, as noted in earlier episodes, some Tommies cut to the chase by throwing in bombs rather than sitting there for hours like a Charlie or a George and getting nothing. This was the plan of Corporal Fred Poulter, a dispatch rider with the Royal Engineers. He chucked a Mills bomb into the River Scarpe near Arras in April 1917.

He had been motivated by the claim of a chum that there was salmon in the river.

Disappointingly, nothing surfaced apart from an old boot. The pal who had claimed the presence of salmon felt that something more drastic was needed and brought along a trench mortar; he blew such a hole in the river that it changed course. There were still no salmon.

Lieutenant-Colonel Liddell of the 4/Coldstream Guards fished in a small canal at Clairmaris near Poperinghe. He believed in a bit of comfort so fished from the orderly room through an open window, with his feet on the window ledge. He landed the odd eel or two. Lieutenant Blacker saw the opportunity for some fun here. He had been making preparations for some time, buying a toy crocodile in the town and filling it with bricks. Creeping stealthily past the orderly room, Blacker attached the crocodile to the end of his CO's line. Liddell, feeling heavy pressure, thought he was about to land a big one, leapt to his feet and hauled away, until the crocodile came flying through the window, spraying bricks in all directions. He was highly amused by the prank, enhancing his reputation as a 'sportsman'. What his attitude would have been if one of the bricks had hit him it's hard to say.

Other 'sportsmen', a medical officer and a subaltern, were chased across muddy fields near Arras, in June 1917, by a handful of villagers who had been lying in wait for persistent poachers. The officers had had success with salmon but their escape was hampered by squirming fish under their tunics.

Rations

Tom MacDonald of the 9/Royal Sussex asked his platoon lieutenant when he could eat his iron rations. 'You can start on them when your belly button hits your backbone and your hip bones stick out of your trousers,' the subaltern advised him smartly.

The 11/South Wales Borderers attacked Contalmaison on 7 July 1916 and, on this occasion, the rations suffered more than the infantry. Sergeant Albert Perryman, in charge of fifty-two men, had one and a half loaves of bread, a piece of muddy boiled bacon, a few hard biscuits, some currants and sultanas and a petrol tin of tea. The thought of Jesus and the feeding of the 5,000 was no consolation to Albert or his men. They picked lots out of a hat and the losers went hungry.

Losing rations on the hazardous journey along the communication trench at night was a perennial nightmare and could lead to strained relations with comrades. Harry Gregg and a fellow private, Walter Brown, with sandbags full of mixed tea, sugar, cheese and jam (at least the jam was in tins), were forced out of the communication trench by dint of the fact that it was full of water. It was rather hairy up top, with shells going in all directions, from friend or foe (it was hard to tell). Gregg and his mate decided to deal with the situation by blaming each other, accompanied by obscene character assassinations.

Eventually, Gregg told Brown to 'sod off' and took a running jump to cross the trench, slinging his sandbags in advance. They both fell in the water and Gregg's language, already reaching heights of which he hardly knew he was capable, lifted a notch further. He also blamed Brown for this and added that Brown had no parents, was witless, and could, as far as Harry was concerned, disappear up one of his own orifices. Brown was struck silent by his pal's scathing attack and also ducked smartly as some shrapnel just missed him ('iron rations' of a different sort). Gregg was wallowing about below trying to find his sandbags.

'Happy Christmas, Harry,' said Brown suddenly; Gregg doubled up with laughter and Brown joined in, jumping in the water and pretending to swim. They got back safely with their (wet) sandbags and the ties that bound them were stronger than ever.

Lieutenant Duffin (Royal Horse Artillery) could be forgiven for thinking that the steak he had bought for lunch to entertain his fellow officers was also made of iron. When fellow gunner Lieutenant Tyndale-Biscoe arrived for the meal Duffin was standing on top of a barrel and leaping down on a plank. 'What on earth are you doing?' enquired the guest.

'Trying to soften up this bloody meat. It's under the plank,' revealed Duffin. 'It must have died of extreme old age.'

A Royal Engineer cook, at Foncquevillers (4 January 1916), must have had a slice off the same beast. He was surveying it, wondering what to hit it with, when the nose cap of a small shell flew through the window, missed him and the beef and broke a pile of plates. He was philosophical. 'Pity it didn't hit the bloody beef,' he observed. 'I need summat to make an impression on it.'

At least the meat was dead. Men of the 1/Cameron Highlanders, on the run from Jerry in April 1918, and very short of food, were delighted to come across two live and fat pigs in Esars. But killing a pig was not part of their military training. Yet they were pretty determined to do it and John Jackson recorded that the methods employed to dispatch these two beasts he 'would not care to describe'. All he would say was that they 'met a soldier's death'.

A vital ingredient in iron rations was hard 'dog' biscuits, very good at filling up empty stomachs but a menace to teeth. They were so often referred to as 'those f***ing biscuits' that the padre of the 2/RWF advised his CO to place a guard outside the canteen to prevent any biscuit committing an act of gross indecency.

Tea

Tea was another staple part of iron rations. In fact, Sidney Rogerson believed that tea was the reason for the ultimate British victory. He had the idea for colossal banners inscribed 'Tea: 1914–1918' to be waved at victory parades to inform the celebrating crowds that this is what did it. However, the problem with tea, apart from the water used to make it (tasting of chloride of lime and petrol), was its varying hue. Second Lieutenant C.M. Slack (4/East Yorkshires) commented on 9 February 1916 that he was often unsure whether he was drinking coffee or tea, or something else. He was usually offered something that was traditionally light brown, but he also had experience of black liquid (even with milk in it) and sometimes green. Taste, nevertheless, tended not to vary. The best way that Slack could describe its flavour was 'dead men'.

Which was why George Weeks should not have been surprised at his experience when on a detachment near Kitchener Wood (St Julian) late in 1917. They were out there trying to construct a foundation for a machine intended to locate Big Bertha, an enormous enemy gun firing on Paris. They were not having a lot of success: it was so wet that every time they dug out some liquid earth it rapidly filled in again and trapped unwary Pioneers in a vice-like grip. They had to be dragged out with pulleys and had to leave their waders behind, and sometimes their trousers too.

Anyway, they were served up with some tea and it was blue. Understandably, they were a bit cautious and requested that the cook show them where he had acquired the water. Obligingly, he took them to a nearby crump hole. In it was floating a Jerry corpse. George and his mates decided to lay off the blue tea until they were really thirsty.

Another dubious source of water was that used by Private Thomas McCall, a Cameron Highlander. No petrol tins full of water had arrived so McCall folded the tarpaulin roof of his dugout to catch the rain water. The resulting reservoir also had interesting colours and some wriggling occupants. McCall was not terribly impressed but went ahead and boiled some and made his officer's tea. No complaints surfaced and McCall, who had not partaken, decided to wait for the petrol tins to arrive. He was having a kip when Private Waller woke him and offered him some steaming, hot tea. McCall, really thirsty by this time, gulped it back. 'Christ, that was good,' he sighed in contentment.

'I think it was those wriggly things that gave it a decent flavour,' reckoned Waller. McCall chased him up the trench.

Even More Flavour

Back on the topic of flavour, Sapper Arthur Sambrook's stove (trenches near Loos in 1916) was constructed from a large ex-paint drum. The flue leading the fumes out of his dugout was a pole with a biscuit tin hammerer around it. He was up above one day whilst his mates huddled round the stove. He had in his hand a festering slice of mature Camembert and decided to experiment to see what the odour would be like if it was dropped down the pipe on to the steaming stove. He was quite interested to detect wild shouts from below: 'Gas! F***ing gas! Get your helmets on, lads!'

Flavours abounded on the Western Front. It was, for some Tommies, the overwhelming memory they had of the trenches. Moreover, they claimed that every trench had its distinctive smell; not surprising when you consider the potential range of ingredients: latrines, corpses, chloride of lime, body sweat and other personal odours, stinking clothes, gas lurking in the hollows of no-man's-land (even in the trench if there was no wind to blow it away – they sometimes tried to do this with fans), cordite, pink mud and dead rats, etc. etc.

TWELVE

Three Sheets to the Wind

'Three sheets to the wind' was the old soldiers' phrase for drunk, inebriated, sozzled, paralytic, totally out of it, and the rest. The source of this term is nautical – 'sheets' meaning ropes. If these were not properly attached to the sail it would flap around wildly and the boat would lurch about. 'Three sheets' was the capsizing stage.

One sheet to the wind implied only tipsiness. Early (and later) experiences of French beer – that pale and insipid stuff – suggested to Tommy that even getting to this point was difficult. Their estimates of the amount needed for inebriation varied. At St Quentin on 27 August 1914 the 2/RWF had already assessed the potency of French beer, or lack of it. One Fusilier calculated that the dose needed was ten bottles – and that was only one sheet to the wind. Alfred Burrage put it at 242 pints.

However, obviously, the French did have something to offer serious drinkers. The Royal Irish Fusiliers were in the Somme area in November 1915 when four warrant officers and senior sergeants became dead drunk in an *estaminet* on brandy doped with pure alcohol – known as 'French firewater', and strictly illegal. They were so ill they were taken to hospital. Indeed, senior NCOs appeared as the main experts when it came to what to drink in France and Flanders. Privates often followed their lead, although they tended to have less money than the 'Sar'nts'. Quartermasters and their assistants were famous for surrounding themselves with ample supplies of varied booze. In *The BEF Times* for 15 August 1917 there was an item entitled: 'Our Short Story. There was once a teetotal Quartermaster. The End.'

At the other end of the scale, there was booze deprivation because of serious breaks in cash supply. This hit many drinkers on non-pay days. On pay days they went out and spent the lot on drink, leaving a bleak run of nine or so dry days unless something could be begged, borrowed or stolen. Some committed drunkards managed to get loans out of young and inexperienced subalterns, even though they were already in serious debt to the army. One soldier, offered only a loan of 5 francs by one such chinless wonder, told him to 'Keep it and spend it on a f***ing rocking horse' – with the result that he spent many drinkless hours tied to a wagon wheel.

Front-Line Duty & Rum

Drinking alcohol in the trenches was discouraged for obvious reasons. Other ranks were not (officially) allowed to drink spirits anywhere (except rum) and carrying crates of beer up the communication trench was difficult. However, there were cases of drunk soldiers (and officers) in trenches. This was sometimes connected with the rum ration. Putting someone like Private McNaught in charge of the rum ration (New Year's Day, 1915) was a grave error, since dawn found him stumbling about in no-man's-land, swearing at the Germans who were laughing uproariously. The company commander screamed at McNaught; there was more bad language and then McNaught fell headlong into the trench.

'SRD' was stamped on the side of the rum jars, or 'grey hens' as they were known. It meant 'Special Rations Department' officially but to the troops 'Seldom Reaches Destination'. Corporal P.J. Clarke (13/Rifle Brigade) provided graphic evidence of this process. As he reached each group of men the sergeant dishing it out enquired: 'Had your rum yet? No? Here you are, then. I think I'll have mine, too, now.' On he'd go to the next group and say exactly the same. By the time he reached the last platoon he struggled to extract a dessert-spoonful for each man (which, anyway, was well below the official ration) and also to stand up. They must have all known what he was up to but it was not worth their while doing anything about it.

Trooper Albert 'Smiler' Marshall (Essex Yeomanry) was attached to 170 Tunnelling Company for a time and he reckoned there was a lot more rum underground than on the surface. Indeed, according to him, he was given so much of it he rubbed some on his feet. As a result, he claimed he had the best pair of feet in the army.

'SRD' had other histories as well: a gunnery commander, Major Pargiter, called up the adjutant (Arthur Behrend). 'You know the rum jars you kindly sent us this afternoon?'

'You mean the ones the colonel told you not to open until we get on the move again?'

'Yes, but that's not the point. The point is that those rum jars do not contain rum. They contain nut oil for Chinese labourers' feet.'

Champagne

According to many Tommies, the right amount of poison gas drifting across *la zone rouge* could simulate the effects of a bottle of champagne. However, it was a delicate task calculating what the optimum strength needed to be for this effect. Not many of them took a gamble on it. Some old soldiers did delay donning their gas helmet in the hope of getting the right sort of whiff.

It was the view of the 'Old Soldier' of 2/RWF (expressed, for instance, in the trench at Laventie in July 1915) that the ideal way to leave the trenches was horizontally – but dead drunk not dead. He said this as he watched one of his comrades being carted off to the aid post following the discovery of a chest full of wine exposed whilst extending the trench, which included several bottles of champagne.

Lieutenant-General Hunter-Weston came across such a horizontal warrior in June 1917, assumed the worst and saluted 'the brave dead' – 'Wassa ole bugger goin' on 'bout?' mumbled the 'corpse'.

The 1/Northumberland Hussars found a cellar crammed with champagne in Gheluvelt during the First Battle of Ypres in 1914. But this was at a critical time in the conflict and the Hussars had to make a quick getaway. Hastily, they stuffed four bottles each into the strapping around their saddles and charged west up the Menin Road. But this gave the champagne a rare shaking and the corks started exploding in all directions and the golden fluid poured down the flanks of the horses.

The 8/Leicesters were introduced to champagne in September 1915 at Berles-au-Bois but, unfortunately, on the very night they had to march back to the trenches. They were all over the place and the Welsh corporal in charge of them, who had not had any champagne and also disliked English privates, gave vent to his feelings: 'Carry your liquor like the f***ing English, you are!' he roared, half in anger and half in envy. What he didn't know was that they still had bottles of the stuff hidden about their persons. They were allowed to lie down to sleep when they arrived at the front, which provided them with the opportunity to consume their extra bottle of champagne.

Private Read remembered little about events of the previous night in the morning but the fact that he was covered in cake crumbs, raisins and chewed sandbags helped him to recall that he had received a parcel from home and hung it above his head before finishing the champagne. The rats had done the rest.

More Drunks

Charles Edmonds happened upon a ration party one night in a communication trench. They were comatose in a dugout, having seen off the whole rum ration for a company. He tried to stir them and the odd one or two burst into song or ribald shouting. He couldn't do anything with them. An enemy bombardment was in progress so anything heroic was not feasible. His main inclination was to start laughing. He decided to do this and the platoon tried to emulate him but one or two vomited and the rest went back to sleep. He decided to join them and wait until the morning to et stern with them. 'Give ush a kish, sir,' slurred one before resuming his coma.

There were a few drunken officers in the line. During the Allied advance in 1918 the 4/Royal Sussex received a new officer – a Captain Lewis. Now Lewis was exorbitantly fond of rum – could not get enough of it. Soon after his arrival his CO and the adjutant found him asleep at midday whilst his company loafed around doing very little. Stirred from his slumbers, he told his senior officers to 'Bugger off!'

They were lenient about it, putting the offence down to stress, and decided to give Lewis another chance. But it was his last chance. Trying to win back a decent reputation, Lewis offered to find a way around an enormous mine crater named 'Spanbrok Molen'. But while attempting to edge round the colossal depression he fell down into it and became entangled in barbed wire, uttering great volleys of obscenities. With bullets now whistling past their ears, a group of men managed to drag him out, his clothes in tatters, still swearing and stinking of rum.

He was snoring again at midday the following day but, luckily for him, senior officers did not come calling. His men thought he was a right scream. It was easy to serve under him – as long as the Germans didn't attack. They continued to protect him. But Lewis was his own worst enemy; he finished up back at base, running errands for the brigadier. Perhaps he wasn't as daft as he seemed.

Hoards

Hoards of booze hidden, abandoned or lost by French or Flemish citizens, were not uncommon in the desperate circumstances of 1914, and also in 1915 when thousands of citizens became refugees. Thereafter, the treasures faded away but resurfaced during the retreat of the Germans in 1918; except, as we saw earlier, they tended to reside in Expeditionary Force Canteens rather than French cellars.

But the large quantity of stout discovered by the 1/Cameron Highlanders in the deserted homes in Esars on 13 April 1918 was reminiscent of the 1914 treasure troves. The Military Police arrived to supervise its removal to a safe haven (if anywhere was safe from thirsty Tommies). However, the response from the Highlanders was typical – 'What stout?'

Search as frantically as they could, the police could not find the stout. Short of this evidence, the Highlanders could not be accused of pinching it. The MPs had got there pretty smartly so there had not been time to drink it, even at the Highlanders' rate of consumption. It was, in fact, hidden away in the ammunition boxes sitting right in front of the rozzers' noses.

This battalion was in Nieuport Bains on 22 June 1918. Their luck was still in because a shell just missed some of them and landed on a house, revealing a large quantity of wine in the cellar. The CO appointed a select guard from the battalion to watch over it and there wasn't a drop left by morning.

Perhaps the colonel had forgotten the episode of the barrel of white wine 'found' on the St Quentin–Amiens road at Marielière in the previous year (May 1917). By the time officers came round to inspect it the barrel was empty. But concealing a whole barrel of wine within minutes proved even beyond the ingenuity of the 1/ Cameron Highlanders. Every container they had was filled to the brim with the booze. However, the thirsty men could not wait to sample the quality of the *vin blanc* and on parade the fumes became overpowering. Those who eventually received field punishments consoled themselves with the fact that they had drunk more wine than the others.

The Royal Irish Rifles were still in the English Channel when they started breaking into the liquor store on the steamer and stealing shelves of spirits and beer. Military Police went round questioning everybody. 'What liquor store?' was the standard response.

Officers and other ranks at ports and base camps reputably did well for drink. The Artists' Rifles docked at Le Havre in March 1917 and were inspected by a Brass Hat who stumbled out of a guard hut stinking of whisky. He stared blearily at the Artists. 'Y're a dishgrace to y're Reg't, whoever you are,' he muttered, and staggered back into the hut.

Billets

Once in the rest areas, old soldiers and Kitchener volunteers alike could seek nightly oblivion as long as the cash lasted out. In January 1918 the peace of the night in the village of Gézaincourt, near

Doullens, was shattered by the cries for help of the village priest. He was being assaulted by a drunken gunner who had mistaken him for a lady.

Drink-driving was a problem behind the lines. A lorry ran into the village pond in Watou on 1 May 1915. The ASC driver staggered out of his cab, swam a few strokes (it was a foot deep) and went to sleep on the bank. The 2/Queen Victoria Rifles helped themselves to his lorry-load of loaves.

Drink was behind the bulk of the 'crimes' committed at rest. Offenders re-offended all the time, such as Corporal Bush of the 7th Field Company, Royal Engineers. He got drunk, lost his stripes, returned to the front and was continually praised for initiative and valour, regaining his rank. But On 12 May 1917, at an *estaminet* in Humbercourt, Bush was refused a drink on the grounds that he was already drunk. As was his wont, he became overtly aggressive – not a wise thing to do because the *estaminet* was next door to the sergeant's mess. A sergeant hung out of the window and told him to clear off. 'Shut your mouth!' blared Bushy, 'or I'll push your head through the f***ing window!'

Next day he became Private Bush once again. The following week he was crimed for being dead drunk in a pig sty and the CO, losing patience, sent him up for a court martial. There, he was sentenced to nine months in military prison. He served this, came back to his company and served with such gallantry that his sentence was expunged from the records and he became Corporal Bush once more. Whether he stayed that way is a matter for research.

There were merry parties, especially those of Highland divisions, at the New Year. On 1 January 1916 John Jackson (6/Cameron Highlanders) held up the piper, Willie Hamilton, who was incapable, whilst he rendered his favourite tune, *Auld Robin Grey*.

377 Battery, Royal Artillery, was moving up to the Battle of Cambrai in November 1917. Because so many troops were on the move (probably 100,000 or more), logistics were strained and the gunners were very short on rations. At least the officers had the 'caravan'. This was a decrepit ex-gypsy vehicle crammed with whisky. It was so rickety that the weight of hundreds of bottles seemed likely to undo it at any moment. The major topic of conversation amongst the artillery was not 'What's going to happen at Cambrai?' but 'Is

the caravan all correct?' So often was this desperate enquiry made that by the time they got to within 5 miles of their destination it was indelibly etched on the gunnery officers' minds. Forevermore, instead of the usual question of 'You okay?' there was 'How's the caravan?' In fact, it never reached Cambrai but collapsed under its burden. Whatever happened to the whisky is another matter for research. Newcomers to the battery in later years were always mystified when asked, 'How's your caravan?' Whisky was that important. When *The Wipers Times* announced the possibility that whisky could be banned on the Western Front, its very popular response was, 'No whisky, no war'.

THIRTEEN

Live & Let Live

A German Wipers Times

Trench warfare developed its own style of 'live and let live'. It was impossible to wage this attrition unless there were tacit agreements to go quiet at times. Otherwise, men and materiel would have soon worn out. The foot soldiers were all for it. Commanders looked forward to the next offensive but had to accept something less aggressive in the meantime. Officers in the field were frequently urged to be as 'offensive' as possible, e.g. night raids to keep Jerry on his toes, sometimes with the bonus of a prisoner or two to interrogate. Vigilance was de rigueur but so was developing co-operative tactics with the enemy.

Allied and German trenches were comparatively near each other, in some cases not a lot more than 20 metres apart. It's quite instructive these days to visit the lines at the foot of Vimy Ridge (Arras) to see how close they were. Thus, verbal communication was not difficult. There was a lot of shouting across no-man's-land and many Germans could speak decent English. It was because of this that Tommy soon realised that Fritz had a sense of humour and it wasn't a lot different to his own. There is evidence of a sort of German *Wipers Times* – trench magazines and newspapers. There was an intriguing little piece in *Jenaer Volksblatt* at Christmas time in 1914. It was entitled 'A Christmas onslaught on to the Field-Grey':

Yesterday at four in the afternoon [there was] a fierce and terrible onslaught of Christmas packages into our trenches. No man was spared. Not a single package fell into the hands of the French. One suffered the impaling of a salami two inches in diameter straight into his stomach. Another had two raisins from an exploding pastry fly directly into his eye ...

(Quoted in Stanley Weintraub's *Silent Night*.)

Derision

Even before the end of 1914 Jerry had demonstrated an inclination towards ridicule. At Houplines on 19 December the whole British front was ordered to fire a rapid three-round volley to 'wind-up' (make nervous) the Boche. This was designed to deceive the Prussians into thinking that an attack was imminent, in the hope that they would start running about and exposing themselves to the artillery. The ploy just did not work: not only were the Prussians not rattled, but they let go with a cacophony of catcalls, waved flags and threw up showers of turnips, old newspapers and other assorted rubbish over no-man's-land.

The British soldiers also soon detected amongst their foe the same ironic attitude towards those who had sent them into this battle. In the summer of 1915, at the Cuinchy front line, the Royal Welsh Regiment tried to get a conversation going with Jerry. There was again an ulterior motive: the Welsh had been instructed to try and get some strategic information out of the enemy. Very soon they discovered that the Germans liked the girls living in Cuinchy when they had recently occupied the village. Encouraged, a Welsh called out, 'How's the Kaiser?' They got a standard answer – in the best of health, he was. 'And how's the Crown Prince?'

'Bugger the Crown Prince!' called a German loudly, followed by a lot of laughing (and some protests and argument).

British troops were busy in no-man's-land in front of the Foncquevillers trenches in the early hours of Guy Fawkes' Day later in 1915. As dawn came the Germans found themselves confronted with a life-size effigy hanging on a rope and festooned with mock medals,

Billy Congreve's servant, Private Cameron, poses as a German soldier, complete with a *Flamenwerfer*.

including several enormous Iron Crosses. A large sheet of cardboard on it announced, 'Your bloody Kaiser'. Rockets were concealed all over its person and it was soaked in paraffin. Fuses ran back to the barbed wire. Jerries lined up all day to fire at it and bulls and inners were recorded by flags in both sets of trenches and there was a lot of shouting and laughing. The kaiser steadfastly refused to go up in flames and it was left to a couple of grenades tossed by those who had constructed him to do the job, and the resulting conflagration was greeted by tumultuous cheering from both sides.

Something similar had been attempted from the air on April Fools' Day earlier in 1915. A Royal Flying Corps bomber flew over Lille airfield and dropped ... a football. German ground personnel ran in all directions as the ball bounced in their direction. When it didn't explode they approached it very warily. There was writing on it: 'April Fool. Gott Strafe England.'

Notices from the Saxons

Tommy was to learn that not all Germans were the same. To the Prussians the Saxons were foreigners and they treated them as such. The Saxons provided a lot of fun for the British with their funny notices. As the Prussians were being bombarded near Armentières, on 27 January 1915, neighbouring Saxons sat on their parapet and cheered hits on the Prussians. They didn't like the Bavarians either and put up a sign: 'The Bavarians are replacing us tonight. Wait till then, Tommy, and then shoot the bastards.'

Later in the year, on 4 June, Saxons were opposite the 1/4 Oxon and Bucks Light Infantry at Ploegsteert Wood and were being relieved by the Prussians. The message this time was more or less the same: 'The Prussians are coming here tonight. Give it to them hot tomorrow.'

There were frequent observations about the quality of the British marksmanship and ammunition. The Germans were top-notch on night illumination. They loved sending up flares all night long and they were always very bright. Early British attempts were poor by comparison. Efforts in early 1915 were greeted with cheers from the Saxons, and at Armentières on 5 February the classic shout was:

'Why not try a match?' However, by Christmas 1915 the standard had improved and the Saxon comments at Armentières became more complimentary: 'That's a bloody good light, sir!'

There were equally disparaging remarks about early British poison gas. The first attempts to poison the Germans were at Loos in September 1915. It was planned as a surprise and so a huge security operation was set in motion (but trying security on Jerry was very often a flop). Sadly, progress was hindered by three windless days and the Saxons put up a series of trench notices: 'Wind still wrong for your damned gas, sir.' – 'Hard luck, Tommy, still trying to poison us?' – 'Why not try some bellows?' – 'If you Tommies all stand in a row and give one big puff you might still do it.'

By the time of the Battle of the Somme, notices in the German trenches were fewer and struck a more sombre note. As the massive bombardment preceding the battle was about to commence, some of them near Thiepval stuck up a board: 'When your bombardment starts we are going to bugger off back 5 miles. Kitchener is buggered. Asquith is buggered. You're buggered. We're buggered. Let's all bugger off home.'

Christmas Truce, 1915

There were not many unofficial truces at Christmas 1915, unlike the previous year. One Jerry decided on a one-man truce, or at least an attempt to come across to the British line and wish them 'Happy Christmas'. He crawled across no-man's-land right up to the British wire. Private Dick Trafford (1/9 King's Liverpool Rifles) was sent out to see what he wanted (Jerries sometimes came across to surrender).

'Are you surrendering?' Trafford called to him. 'You know, Kamerad sort of thing?'

'No – just wishing you all a Happy Christmas, Tommy,' explained the enterprising and festive Fritz. 'Happy Christmas.'

Trafford turned round to convey the news back to his trench. 'He just wants to say Happy Christmas.'

'Tell him Happy Christmas, too,' ordered the lieutenant. 'Then tell him to bugger off.'

Cartoon by W. Heath Robinson.

Trafford carried out his orders: 'Happy Christmas, Fritz, now bugger off.'

Which is what Fritz did; but when dawn came Trafford and his mates saw a hand waving above the German parapet. They waved back.

The Mood Changes

There were not many reports of any truces at Christmas 1916, after the Battle of the Somme, and even fewer a year later. Tolerance reached a low level after the dirty tricks of the retreat to the Hindenburg Line, north and east of the Somme battlefield in the spring of 1917. As they withdrew, the Germans laid waste to the towns and countryside they were leaving behind. True, it was military strategy to destroy anything of potential use to the enemy, but things like booby traps in rum jars, under tin hats, behind stoves, etc. were set to destroy any feelings of empathy on the part of the ordinary British infantrymen.

Their sense of irony had not deserted the Germans, however – seen in messages and drawings left behind for the British to see. The 1/8 Royal Warwickshires found one in Halle: 'Great British advance. Many villages taken' (which indicated that the enemy was well aware of how the British press at home portrayed the war – perhaps their papers did the same). 'Haig takes Halle. 4,000 Germans captured – official', read another one.

So Kind

Happily, there was still a joke or two left, calculated to amuse the British. Lieutenant-Colonel Feilding wrote home to his wife on 15 December 1917 to recount the adventures of his medical officer, who had got himself into a bit of a pickle. The doctor had been attempting to return to the front with the mess-cart piled high with provisions. He drove straight into the German sector. The next day the doctor and the cart were returned to Feilding with the following note: 'Thank you very much for all the good things you have sent us. They will be most useful. So will the good doctor, when he gets sober.'

The MO, in fact, had had a great time over there. He had been entertained royally by his kind hosts with dinner and a lot of wine and schnapps. Being a non-combatant, they had to return him; the doctor never forgot German hospitality.

It was in the same month when, short of rations, Feilding's gunnery battery all rushed for their rifles when some wild ducks flew overhead. The Germans started shooting at them as well, but it was the gunners who bagged one of the birds. Unfortunately, it fell on the German side. A notice went up immediately: 'Thank you so much. Most kind.'

There was another story just like the one featuring Feilding's MO. 'Jumbo' was another medical officer in the Ypres Salient. Jumbo liked his daily stroll but his sense of direction did not match his medical skills and on one occasion he contrived to wander into the German lines. The reception was not as good as that accorded to the other MO because they thought he was a spy in disguise, and threatened him with a revolver and a couple of bayonets. He was terrified inside but his fat, wrinkly and wobbly face appeared to the Germans to indicate a detached amusement. This apparently brave coolness impressed them tremendously. After a brief discussion they decided unanimously that he was really a doctor and someone's suggestion that he should be adopted as their regimental mascot was taken up with enthusiasm.

So, like the other MO, they gave him a very nice dinner with lots of champagne and sent him back, along with a big French dog and a cart. They turned out in force to see him off with many an invitation to come over at any time and have dinner.

Football Results

The British continued to receive reminders about how good German intelligence about them was, particularly concerning what battalion was guarding what front. They even knew the identity of individual Tommies. On 27 July 1916 on the Somme front the Bradford Pals endured heavy shelling and numerous casualties. Many prisoners were also taken. Later, one of the German boards was thrust high above the parapet: 'You paid £1,000 for Dickie Bond. We got him for nothing.' Dickie Bond was the centre forward for Bradford City and this transfer fee was an extremely high one for those times. German knowledge of English football came from the fact that many of them had worked in England before the war.

Fritz the 'bunmaker' called out at Armentières in March 1915: 'It is I, Fritz the Bunmaker, of London. What is the football news?' Fritz, in general, was interested in the English football results, especially for London teams. In the summer of 1915 someone shouted to the 18/Londons at Cuinchy: 'What about the Cup Final?'

'Chelsea lost,' a London fan informed him (rather cheerfully – he must have been an Arsenal supporter).

'Hard luck,' sympathised Herman.

'He must be a darned good sort of a sausage-eater,' remarked a real Chelsea fan.

Intelligence

In the Houplines sector just before Christmas 1914, a Prussian played the British national anthem on a cornet accompanied by a chorus. For the Tommy, it was a weird experience to hear Germans singing *God Save our Gracious King*. However, this rendition was followed by a huge shout of: '*Hoch der Kaiser!*' The Tommies, rather disappointed at this turn of events, retorted loudly, 'F*** the Kaiser!'

But it was the Prussians who had the last laugh: 'When are you going back to Maryhill Barracks?' shouted the cornet player.

Also at the time of the truces in 1914, when men of the London Rifle Brigade were actually chatting to some Jerries in no-man's-land, one of them was carrying a placard reading: '*Gott mit uns.*' There were hurried discussions in the ranks of the Londoners and someone found a bit of board and the inevitable purple pencil, and the result was this: 'We got mittens too.'

There were many personal messages floating across no-man's-land. Lieutenant Eberle of the 2nd Field Company, Royal Engineers, heard one at Ploegsteert Wood: 'Hello, the Gloucesters! What are they saying about you in Bristol? When is this war going to stop? I have a wife and four children in Flax Bourton.'

Major H.L.M. Tritton of the Essex Yeomanry reported a similar incident for April 1915. 'Are you Varvicks?' came a rather plaintive cry across no-man's-land. A battalion of the Royal Warwickshires was indeed next to the Essex Yeomanry. 'Yes,' a Brummie replied politely.

'I've a widow and two childs in Birmingham.'

The Brummie became less polite. 'If you don't stick that square head of yours out of sight you will have a widow and also two orphans in Birmingham.'

Sometimes, with their superior information, Fritz became cocky. In the Loos Salient in 1916 the names of the battalions being relieved were shouted across. However, they didn't know who was coming in that evening: 'Who's relieving you, Tommy?'

Someone was quick to shout back, 'Fursst Black Watch an' th' Oirish Guards.'

These were the most feared regiments in the whole British Army and a respectful hush fell upon the enemy trenches. The Black Watch and the Irish Guards were not likely to exchange pleasantries with the Jerries.

They always seemed to be aware of the presence of Bantam battalions, which consisted of very short men. An official order of 31 January 1916 read: 'It is notified that until further notice only men who are between five feet and one inch and five feet and four inches in height are to be considered for Bantam Battalions.' Whenever the Germans spotted them there were mass catcalls of 'Cock-a-doodle-do' from their ranks.

Services & More Presents

Many Tommies amused themselves by shouting, 'Waiter!' This was an allusion to the fact that there were a lot of ex-London waiters over there. The usual response was for dozens of heads to pop up above the parapet calling, 'Coming, sir.'

During the Christmas truce of 1914 ex-barbers gave the other side haircuts. Bruce Bairnsfather watched a man from his battalion providing this service, using an empty ammunition box for a chair. During one of the truces a soldier of the 3/London Rifles recognised a Saxon as the barber who used to cut his hair in High Holborn. 'And now,' Herman declared cheerfully, 'I give you short back and sides vunce more. I get my scissor.' As promised, he went and fetched his equipment and also sat the Londoner down on an ammunition box (empty, of course). As he neared the end of the operation he produced the traditional open razor to complete the job. 'And now,' he announced, 'I cut your throat – it vill save ammunition tomorrow.'

Nearby, a German juggler (this was near Armentières) set up his table in no-man's-land and went through his complete repertoire of tricks. A large, appreciative audience of British and German soldiers gave him an enthusiastic hand.

The *Daily Express* only a week before had reported an incident where the Saxons slipped a very nice chocolate cake into a British trench, explaining that it was their captain's birthday. They asked for a cessation of hostilities on the next day between 7.30 p.m. and 8.30 p.m. so that a party could be held in honour of their officer. Candles and footlights were to be lit at 7.30 and it would be safe for the Tommies to put their heads above the parapet at that hour.

The Tommies sent a message back with a gift of tobacco. The party was entertained by a band and they were able to join in the choruses of British tunes, such as *My Old Dutch*. But a rather unfriendly Tommy, less happy about all this fraternisation, yelled out: 'We'd rather die than sing in German.'

A big voice boomed back: 'It will kill us if you do.'

Some deals were struck during the truces. Brothers Frank and Maurice Wray of the 5/London Rifle Brigade were presented with a pickelhaube helmet in exchange for some bully beef and Tickler's plum and apple jam. However, Frank received a later call from his new friend asking to borrow back the helmet as it was needed for an inspection. He promised to return it the next day. He was as good as his word, and there was also some schnapps. The brothers took across some more corned beef (glad to get rid of it, but the Jerries liked it).

It was only a few days after Christmas when a Jerry, trying to take advantage of the new-found sense of fraternity, called across to the Londoners. 'I need to get a message through to Miss Jones of 224A, Tottenham Court Road,' he explained.

'I'll go and see her, all right,' replied a saucy Tommy, 'and I'll give her one, all right.'

Even less convivial were the exchanges overheard by Andrew Bowie of the 1/Cameron Highlanders in 1916. '*Deutschland, Deutschland, über alles,*' shouted a patriotic Jerry.

A Scot replied: '*Deutschland, Deutschland, über arseholes.*'

Smiler Marshall of the Essex Yeomanry, a walking treasure trove of stories, said that in 1915 he was in a trench less than 20 metres from the Jerries; so close, in fact, that they used to throw over un-fused stick grenades to each other with presents attached. One with two fags hit Smiler on the head and he sent it back with a whole packet of fags.

Target Practice

As noted in the Guy Fawkes' Day encounter, both sides frequently put up targets for the other side to aim at. Captain Billie Nevill actually crawled out into no-man's-land at night in November 1915 and stuck up a series of German flags in the crump holes. Next morning, obligingly, the Germans started firing at the flags and Billie signalled bulls' eyes, inners and magpies with a white flag. Lieutenant-Colonel Feilding's sniping officer (6/Connaught Rangers) told him that usually when he missed his intended victim signalled a 'miss' by raising and lowering a stick above the parapet.

A bored sentry of the 8/Leicesters at Monchy-au-Bois (September 1915) stuck his cap on a bayonet and lifted it high above the parapet. There was a sharp double crack and the cap sailed on to the parados (rear bank of the trench). Someone printed 'Bull' on an old French notice board and there was appreciative laughter from the marksman and his pals.

Music

Music was provided by both sides. During the Second Battle of Ypres, in April 1915, Private Ernest Todd recalled the efforts of 'Cornet Joe', as they called him. This fellow could play any British tune they chose to request, resulting in many a spirited sing-a-long session, the favourite being *Down by the Old Bull and Bush*. A 'Company Band' of the Coldstream Guards (Béthune, August 1915) played *Die Wacht am Rhein* followed by *Rule Britannia* and *God Save the King*, and German listeners clapped and cheered and shouted, 'Encore!'

The accordion player from the German trenches at Monchy-au-Bois, in September of the same year, was the great favourite of the 8/Leicesters, who particularly loved his rendition of *Goodbye, Dolly Gray*. They called 'Bravo!' and 'Encore!' Their reward was *Down by the Old Bull and Bush*.

The Leicesters were so impressed they called out, 'What's your name, Jerry?'

'Charlie – you bloody English bastards!' came the rather uncharitable response. While the Leicesters were trying to think of a suitable reply, he added, '*Gut nacht!*' followed by a couple of bullets which smacked into the Leicesters' parados. 'Charlie' obviously liked playing, but not the British very much. Private Freddie Smith disagreed. 'He likes us,' he commented. Perhaps they asked for it – the Leicesters – because after they called, 'Encore!' at Béthune in August, they opened up with every rifle, mortar and bomb to hand. They might have been trying to play the *1812 Overture*.

Curious Incidents

There were a number of curious incidents arising from all this fraternisation. A Scottish battalion was quite taken aback in early 1915 when about twenty Jerries emerged from their trench and started mowing the long grass in front of it. Admittedly it was a very quiet front, but they were taking a chance because no prior notice of the event had been indicated. They obviously had confidence in the fair play of the Scots. The truth was simpler, however: the Scots command was pleased to see the long grass go because it had been providing cover for potential enemy raids.

On 6 August 1916 a German soldier wandered out into no-man's-land in order to stick up a list on the barbed wire of British prisoners they had captured. Seeing no one about, he brought the list even closer to the British trenches. As he came forward, however, a British patrol emerged from a shell hole in front of him. He was unable to speak English very well and so his explanation of what he was doing didn't get through. Usually, in these circumstances, Jerries would be trying to surrender. His attempted mime – putting his hands above his head and then shaking it vigorously – was no more successful than his linguistic efforts. But really the patrol couldn't let him go, even if they had understood what he was doing, because he was too near the British line not to have seen all sorts of things which his commanders would be interested in.

The story had an interesting ending: Brigade found out what the Jerry had intended to do and took a sympathetic line. They got the Royal Flying Corps to drop a note over enemy lines with the poor blighter's name and an explanation as to why they couldn't let him go. They also sent thanks for the list of prisoners. Live and let live.

In their final desperate attacks in the summer of 1918, the German army also turned to very short men, even dwarfs. One of these specimens, sporting a helmet which fell down over his eyes, surrendered to Captain C.P. Blacker of the 2/Coldstream Guards. He was well prepared: in his pack he had a white flag with a red cross on it. Their main objective was to surrender as soon as possible.

The French

The Tommies developed a soft spot for French kids and tried to give them spare food whenever they could. For their part, some of these children were enterprising salesmen – anything from newspapers to their sisters. Robert Graves arrived in Le Havre early in 1915 and was immediately surrounded by numerous small boys. 'I take you to my sister,' one of them offered. 'She very nice. Very good jig-a-jig. Not much money. Very cheap. Very good. I take you now. Plenty champagne for me.'

Up near the front line Graves came across more of them selling the continental edition of the *Daily Mail*. 'Bloody good news for the

Poilu : " Allumette ? "
Tommy : " 'Allo, mate." (Shakes.)

Published by kind permission of the family of Bert Thomas.

Ingleese! Bloody good news! Ten more Ingleese ships sunk! Bloody good news for the Ingleese!'

A persistent urchin in Harfleur on 12 July 1916 accosted the Queen Victoria Rifles: 'Gimme fag, bloody Tommie. Gimme bleedin' chocklick.'

Little girls were not necessarily any politer. 'Bonjour, ma petite,' a general greeted a sweet little thing with blonde ringlets in Locre. 'Garn, fat arse!' responded the vision.

Behind the front lines British soldiers encountered more mature personalities. Graves made the acquaintance of Monsieur Elie Caron in Montague le Fayel. He invited the officer to a meal and, when seated, presented him with a pamphlet entitled '*Comment vivre cent ans*' (How to live a hundred years) when they both knew that the Battle of the Somme was imminent. Graves appreciated the irony.

In the last month of the war George Weeks was in Engelfontaine on the edge of the Mormal Forest (to the east of Cambrai) and became friendly with an elderly citizen (he said he was 86), known locally as 'Old Chicken Eye' (his real name was Francois Bonet). He lived in a tiny cottage amidst the trees. His nickname derived from the black rings around his eyes and also the fact that he never blinked. They made a strange pair – a docker from the Isle of Dogs and a graduate and lecturer of the Sorbonne. Bonet spoke better English than George and was also fluent in German and Dutch. He had a detailed knowledge of London.

He had spent the war making wooden trinkets for the Germans who occupied the area. They left him alone as long as he supplied the presents which the troops sent home to their wives, sweethearts and children. George recalled that the cottage stank of chicken droppings, methylated spirit and engine oil, and certain other unidentifiable pongs. He entertained George and some of his pals to many an afternoon tea and also some delicious stew. George, an expert on stew, could not identify the meat in it. Eventually, his curiosity got the better of him. 'What's the stew made of, Old Chicken Eye?' he enquired, in his usual polite way.

'That, George, is squirrel – you won't find a finer meat.'

George almost spat it out, but he had to admit it tasted very good. What the hell?

Monsieur Bonet had the local forest rights. No one could hunt, remove wood etc. without his say-so. If any Germans usurped this authority they didn't get any nice presents for home, so they learnt to obey. That's how Old Chicken Eye spent his war.

These characters were not always nice. Lieutenant Greenwell (4/Oxon and Bucks Light Infantry) called a M. Dubosc 'a vile old beast'. A typical event occurred on 2 August 1916. Dubosc wandered uninvited into the officers' mess, unkempt and filthy, with a stinking beard down to his navel, speaking raucously in his normal rude manner. The young officers pretended they had too much to do to listen to him. But the old devil was not easily ignored and defiantly pointed out that some officers were not doing anything important and had the time to listen to his daily litany of complaints about their soldiers: walking on his grass, spitting on his path – that sort of misdemeanour.

'You,' he pointed rudely at a 2nd lieutenant, 'you are reading a newspaper. You' (at another subaltern eating gooseberries), 'you are only eating. You must listen to what I have to say.'

They continued to ignore him and he strode out swearing profusely in French and English. Later he returned with an enormous live goose and cut off its head with a small pocket knife. It was a typically Dubosc rebuke. Greenwell reckoned that the only time Dubosc was reasonable was when he was dead drunk and feeling sorry for himself and remembering his recently deceased wife. Greenwell almost felt sorry for him at these times.

John Easton, a Fusilier subaltern, had dealings with 'Papa' at Embry. Papa was a sort of local noble and manufacturer of contraband tobacco and cigars. Papa was well aware that Easton and other officers knew about his shady business and tried to bribe them with some of his illegal wares. Easton was presented with three black, very spongy objects which had been freshly rolled from leaves hanging up in Papa's barn, and especially gummed together with his spit. Easton told him what he could do with them and threatened to expose his backroom trade. It was a good way of getting some decent red wine and some eggs out of the old devil.

British soldiers were urged, in the many pamphlets handed to them, to cultivate good relationships with the natives. The writer John Hay

Beith (penname Ian Hay), who served as an officer with the Argyll and Sutherland Highlanders, recalled stopping at a small railway station early in 1915. One of his sergeants attempted to carry out his orders by trying to be nice to a French sergeant guarding the station. This was difficult as neither of them could speak the other's language – or very little of it. But they tried hard, relying on ingenuity. They checked on the sharpness of their bayonets and nodded approvingly. They attempted some 'conversation'.

'Verra goody!' said the Scot, believing he was speaking some sort of French.

'Olrigh! Tipperary!' replied the sentry. 'God kill the King!'

Officers were not necessarily much better at the lingo. A French artillery officer conducted an English artillery officer around his observation post. Trouble arose because Monsieur le Capitaine insisted on speaking (very bad) English and the gunnery captain insisted on speaking (very bad) French. Accordingly, neither of them could understand a word the other uttered but refused to admit defeat (March 1916 in the Ypres Salient near Vlamertinghe).

Tommy tended to get on well with the owners of *estaminet*s and cafes, except when they were trying to rip him off. They were especially keen on young, female owners, such as Émilienne in Berles-au-Bois, a great favourite (so was 'Gingair', a flame-haired, tart-tongued hostess at Skindles in Poperinghe). The welcome in both these places was effusive. Émilienne greeted 'her boys' with hugs, kisses and sparkling banter, whilst 'Skinny Liz' and her mother also did their level best to make everybody comfortable, well fed and well watered. They did a roaring trade but did not neglect to bring out the slate when necessary: 'Oui, oui, Émilienne – pay demain matin – tomorrow.'

'All right, Freddie, you not forget.'

Then she caught sight of someone who was behind on his payments. 'Jaques – Jack, you pay tomorrow – you not pay me – *beaucoup fâché avec vous*' (I shall be angry with you). This produced an appreciative roar of laughter from the crowd of Tommies and shouts of, 'We'll see he pays, Émilienne.'

Some French citizens were not so amiable but often they had good reason for their ill temper, particularly during the headlong retreat of the Allies in March 1918, when the fleeing soldiers were short of food. A scowling farmer's wife in Forceville growled: 'Australian coupy poule's throat. Eggs, napoo!'

A farmer refused to lend 377 Battery, Royal Artillery, a scythe to cut down nettles to feed their horses at a time when fodder for them was in short supply (June 1918). The officers were pretty clever: they invited the old boy to dinner. He had not heard that there was no such thing as a free dinner and eagerly accepted the invitation. As well as some decent food, they plied him with oceans of whisky until he became paralytic and they had to carry him home on a GS wagon. His daughter came round early the next morning, worried that her father was '*très malade*' and not responding to her calls. The captain called round to the farm and collected the scythe and presented the daughter with a bottle of whisky for her father. 'When he comes round,' he suggested, 'you give him this. He'll soon be all right.'

Cecil Slack, an officer of the 1/4 East Yorkshires, reported on living conditions at a farm near Le Havre, where he was billeted en route to the front (13 January 1916). He found the local latrine in an open field; it consisted of a deep hole surrounded by a dilapidated shack. He dragged open the flimsy door and discovered Madame squatting there. She apologised profusely, denting the theory that all French farmers' wives were rude.

When Slack was able eventually to take his turn he found it necessary to take a very deep breath before venturing inside. He was advised not to use the shack in windy conditions, but in his view a bit of ventilation would have done some good.

An *estaminet* in Bavincourt near Arras, in the spring of 1917, was run by a 'Madame Cow' (strictly speaking, it sounded something like 'Madame Vache'). The Artists' Rifles were good customers of hers because of her reasonable prices. Madame Cow could also speak good English, usually straight to the point. One young man tended to drink a lot of coffee. 'If you drink any more of that stuff,' she warned him, 'you'll be pissing all night.'

Private Dave Barney was a very regular customer, due to the presence of Madame Cow's two attractive daughters as much as her cheap egg and chips. However, he warned his chums not to venture into Madame's bedroom because of the stink emanating from it. He was also not keen on Madame's frying pans, black as the ace of spades. Many discerning customers preferred to take away eggs and fry them back at the billet rather than eat them from one of these scum-ridden utensils.

In April 1915 Major Moxon was in his battered signal box (his office) at Sotteville near Rouen when a train with a French crew came to a halt outside. They then proceeded to operate the piercing train whistle incessantly. Moxon, who had endured banging and jarring, as well as whistling since 5 a.m., decided he'd had enough. He flung open the window and yelled at the crew, who were sitting on the footplate drinking wine. 'Stop that bloody whistling right opposite my office! Can't you take your blasted train somewhere else, eh?'

The crew shrugged and grinned and the driver significantly touched his head, slid off the footplate and urinated against the signal box wall.

Other Nationals

Lieutenant Mottram, you may recall, had the task of settling disputes with Flemish citizens. Another part of his work was to arrange the requisition of fields for use as football pitches. He never met a Flemish farmer who was happy about this. 'Why,' they demanded in anguish, 'must we lose money for this le fool-ball?'

When Lieutenant-Colonel Jack (1/Cameron Highlanders) encountered his first American officer (7 August 1918), he asked a company commander if his men were good shots. 'Well, sir,' drawled the 'Doughboy' captain, 'I guess they get lots of practice firing at Revenue officers in Arizona.'

Another American officer in 1918 lamented: 'Oh, I'd like to be sitting at the ball game, with me little straw hat on the back of me head, me coat over me arm, and a bag of peanuts between me feet, whistling "Arabie".'

Captain A.V.L. Agius (1/3 Londons) described a Gurkha sentry he served with in 1915. He was called 'Teak Johnnie'. He only came up to Agius' elbow but when he shouted, ''Alt!' and stuck his bayonet in your belly button, he was terrifying.

A funny thing happened to John Reith, transport officer for the 5/Scottish Rifles. On 5 February 1916 he was driving a horse-drawn wagon when a Sikh soldier jumped in the back. He could speak no English but, when Reith's servant offered him a peppermint bull's eye, he popped it into his mouth, gave it a couple of sucks and then crunched it between his teeth. A blissful smile spread across the weather-beaten face and he held out his hand for another one. In fact, he scoffed the whole bag. It was obvious he was hooked on the sweet so the servant, a kind soul, carefully wrote the name of the sweet on a piece of paper. The Sikh nodded vigorously, understanding what it was for.

By the end of 1917 there were more than 100,000 Chinese labourers on the Western Front trying to make up for the grave shortage of manual workers. When it got to the stage of top infantry battalions digging their own trenches something had to be done about it. Not that the Chinese dug any trenches. It was difficult getting them anywhere near the front line. Who can blame them?

Accordingly, hardly a Tommy by this time had not set eyes on a Chinaman clad in what appeared to be floppy blue pyjamas, although as time went on their apparel became more varied as they tended to steal any clothes they could find. Alfred McLelland Burrage (Artists' Rifles) was moving north with his battalion to the Third Battle of Ypres in 1917 when they met Chinese labourers for the first time. He never saw any of them actually working. They appeared to spend most of the day in blissful idleness, hunched over dixies of rice. Indeed, one of them said to him, 'You makee fight, we makee money.'

When it came to stealing things, however, they seemed to be quite active. It was a good idea not to leave anything removable anywhere near them. When they left their transit ships at Le Havre and other ports they were good at taking anything portable ashore. One of them walked off the boat with the top of a pickaxe sticking up suggestively inside his satin trousers; the crew thought it was so hilarious he got away with it.

The British Army had its quota of spivs, many of whom thought that the Chinese were a soft touch for any scam. The 2/RWF were in the market for this sort of caper. One Fusilier tried to flog a broken watch to a group of labourers. But they weren't daft: they could see it wasn't working. 'No bloody bonny-la,' declared their spokesman.

'No bloody goody-la.' The conman threw the watch in the air and they fought over it like dogs.

Arthur Behrend, Royal Artillery, whilst retreating on the outskirts of Doullens on 26 March 1918, encountered groups of Chinese also on the run. Behrend wrote that they behaved like schoolchildren let out of school for the day. They grinned at everyone and everything. They trickled into every *estaminet* they passed. Some had great bundles of possessions on their heads but others seemed to possess nothing except the flimsy clothes they were wearing. A few were actually trying to help French refugees push wheelbarrows or handcarts holding their pathetic belongings. Others ran after the artillery's lorries, desperately hoping for a lift.

On the edge of the town two of them entered a lingerie shop. They were thrown out instantly. They stood on the pavement chattering and gesticulating like angry children. Sometimes they were not so funny. A company of them near Ypres stabbed their disciplinarian British sergeant-major and then marched brazenly into the city. They were already not popular there because of a habit of walking into homes uninvited.

There were also Fijian labour companies. Every member of them appeared to be over 6 feet tall, substantially built and sporting large mops of hair. A British officer spoke to one of these chaps, who was dressed in a loincloth (hopefully this was summertime), employing pidgin English: 'You commee Fiji?'

'Well, actually old boy, I'm a Cambridge graduate and before coming out here I was a barrister in Lincoln's Inn.'

There were Bengal Lancers at Longavesnes on 27 March 1916. It was actually snowing and there they sat, motionless, around an enormous, blazing fire, flames leaping up 6 feet or more. An artillery officer, surveying this circle of men in the middle of the road, in their turbans and surrounded by piles of snow, thought how utterly incongruous this scene was. Only the Western Front could have produced such a weird spectacle.

FOURTEEN

Animals - Round-Up

Dogs

Under this heading, one should not forget 'Dog', the large cart dog which Buffalo Bill tried to employ in Chapter Three. There were dogs everywhere on the Western Front. Harry Patch, the last Tommy to die, remembered countless dogs (and cats) roaming around the ruined cities, towns and villages, often wandering into the battle zones and even into the trenches, usually searching for food but also for human company. Harry said that some of these animals, understandably, were vicious. A bloke who did some building work for him after the war had brought one home from France. If you were left alone with the beast in a room, the only way you could escape was by showing it the teeth of a saw.

The 7/Royal Warwickshires at Foncquevillers in 1915 adopted the practice of taking stray dogs on to the front line to use as listeners, picking up any sounds in no-man's-land. If they heard anyone out there they would start growling but would not bark and give the game away. However, in December 1915 the order went round that no more dogs were to be brought into the trenches in this fashion owing to a number of 'accidents', which included several commanding officers being bitten. Subsequently, many a strange-shaped and lively sandbag was carried along communication trenches by the Warwickshires. Well into 1916 you would be hard put to find any trenches without

Tank officers and their pets at Poperinghe in the summer of 1917.

their resident dogs – either put to military use or kept just as pets. All of them, anyway, tended to become pets given the strong bond which exists between man and dog.

Usually these pets went back to the rest areas with their masters. The CO of the 2nd Field Company, Royal Engineers, described his unit as a 'travelling circus'. As the sappers moved towards Cauchy La Tour near Béthune, on 25 June 1915, they were accompanied by a large, mature dog and a puppy (and a goat).

For their part, the 7th Field Company were led into battle by Nobby, a Yorkshire terrier. Not far behind him was Monty, a little brown and black job. Further back was a fox terrier bitch called Nellie, who always travelled in style on a pontoon bridge mounted on a wagon. No matter how bumpy the road was, she never fell off.

The Germans also naturally adopted dogs. Indeed, some of these pets often changed sides, sometimes more than once. Some, indeed, had homes on both sides and used up a number of their lives moving from trench to trench. It could have had something to do with the standard of food on offer. When Edmund Blunden tried to feed his terrier on W.H. Davies' bully beef, it cleared off in the general direction of east in search of something a bit tastier.

Robert Graves received a note from Germans opposite him concerning a similar incident. The front line here weaved in and out of the brick stacks of Cuinchy, near Béthune. It was the summer of 1915. The message was dispatched on an un-fused grenade: 'We all German Korporals wish you English Korporals a good day and invite you to a good German dinner tonight with beer (ale) and cakes. Your little dog ran over to us and we keep it safe: it because no food with you so it runs to us. Answer in the same way, if you please.'

On 24 June 1916 a dog moved in the opposite direction to the Sheffield Pals (12/The York and Lancasters). The Pals renamed it 'Boche' and took it back to their billets.

Men of the 16/King's Royal Rifle Corps captured a prisoner in no-man's-land. A dog accompanied him: it had the job of sniffing out British patrols. It was also taken prisoner. When Private Robert Renwick and his comrades arrived back in the British line they were accosted by a sentry: 'Halt – who goes there?'

'King's Royal Rifle Corps, a prisoner, and one dog.'

'Does it know the password?'

'Bollocks.'

'That's the one. Pass King's Royal Rifle Corps, one prisoner and one dog with bollocks.' The dog (actually it was a bitch) was adopted and also rechristened as 'Hattie'. She became a great favourite with the Rifles.

Queenie, a big, black retriever, alternated daily between the 2/Queen Victoria Rifles and the Jerries at Carnoy (October 1915). Some dogs had more sense than to hang about trenches. Freeze took up residence in the aid post at Gapenner, near Abbéville, and lived off the fat of the land. Aid posts were generally well stocked. Freeze enjoyed a rich diet of meat, fish, eggs, fruit, custard and sweet biscuits.

Fortunately, not all dogs became strays and the soldiers saw plenty of working animals or pets of farmers and other house-holders, French and Flemish. They seemed to do a lot of barking – not surprising when you consider all the coming and going. One dog in Arras in 1916 never seemed to stop. Two Tommies billeted with its

" . . . A very fed-up dog."

Published by kind permission of the family of Bert Thomas.

owner, a generous and amiable lady, asked Madame why it barked so much. 'Ah,' she replied, *'parce qu'il a un ver solitaire'* (a tapeworm).

'Blimey, Fred!' exclaimed Sid, 'you'd bleedin' well 'owl all the time if you had a big, bleedin' worm stuck in yer gut!'

Horses

Of all animals on the Western Front (with perhaps the exception of mules) horses suffered the most, being constantly employed in or near the front. Many tens of thousands of them were killed. But they were also the source of some fun, with some real characters in their ranks.

The sappers had great need for horses and wagons because of the heavy loads they had to lug around. The 7th Field Company were in bivouacs in a field near Courcelles in July 1915. The horses were in picket lines in a corner but the smartest of them usually found a way of escaping to something a bit more interesting.

At 2 a.m. the captain shooed off a mare trying to eat his pillow. The major had fastened a groundsheet to a rickety old fence and promptly went to sleep underneath it. At 3 a.m. Horse 1 ran straight through it, leaping wildly over the prostrate CO. The fence was the attraction: fences are for leaping over – even at 3 a.m. Horse 2 attempted this and succeeded in knocking half of it down. Horse 3 was cantering around preparing to destroy the rest of it and the major beat a hasty retreat and joined the captain and his half-eaten pillow.

Lieutenant Edwin Vaughan went on a two-week training course at Berles-au-Bois in July 1916. This included riding lessons for subalterns who were novices in this art. However, the only horses available were large, shaggy dray horses. Gliding through the village, the novice subalterns created a sedate scene – but this was soon to alter. Vaughan was riding Thomas, and Thomas suddenly decided he didn't want to be ambling through Berles-au-Bois but would prefer to be munching hay in his stall. He set off in a determined trot in that direction and all the other shires thought this was a very good idea and followed, still in tidy ranks. They were in no hurry and oblivious to the commands and bad language of the subalterns.

At rest in the summer of 1915, in the Ypres Salient, the Royal Horse Artillery held a Sports Day. A favourite event was the mounted tug o' war. Riders let go of their reins and hung on to the rope for dear life. The horses lacked interest in tug o' war, however, and started to wander off. They then became frisky, either performing two-steps with one another or haring round the field. The riders were in danger of being garrotted, strangled or castrated. Happily, these fates befell none of them and their main problem was trying to stop laughing.

The Royal Fusiliers in Doullens in March 1916 were to be inspected by Sir Douglas Haig. His entourage was just about to arrive when Lieutenant Leader's mount, Ginger, like Thomas, wanted to go home and tore off down the lane. The enterprising 2nd Lieutenant Guy Chapman stepped into the breach and marched smartly to the front of the company. He hardly had time to recover his breath when the field marshal picked him out as worthy of a chat. 'And how long have you been in charge of this company, may I ask?' enquired Haig, in his genial manner.

Guy Chapman obviously thrived on honesty. 'About two minutes, sir,' he replied.

John Reith's horse was a beautiful mare called Sailaway, which she often did when tempted by lumps of sugar. She would do anything to get some of these and followed Reith around all day like a dog in the hope of getting some. When he entered his billet in Armentières she waited patiently at the foot of the steps outside. Her other amusing habit was to roll her eyes frenetically when out riding, trying to pretend that something awful was about to be seen or heard. Actually, she could pick out gunfire at enormous distances which meant she was forever rolling her eyes. 'Silly Sailaway,' grunted Reith fondly, and she swung her head round and round in protest.

Snuffles was Lieutenant Eberle's horse. He was fast and hated being tied up. He broke every head-collar they put on him and stood there and smiled after he had thrown the latest offender aside. In August 1916 Snuffles became unwell – apparently the equestrian version of trench fever. But by September he had fully recovered and celebrated by depositing the groom in the road.

Lieutenant Mottram was given an old horse to ride for his dealings with the Flemish citizens. Mottram's servant named the old beast 'Roundabout' because he had spent most of his life in fairgrounds. Roundabout was grey and weary and stone deaf. The servant reckoned that if you looked closely into Roundabout's eyes you could see he had hundreds of stories to tell you – he had been round about for a long time.

Private George Weeks (24/Queen's) acquired a horse, not usual for a Pioneer. It just appeared one day and gratefully accepted a carrot. George called him Fetlock. Fetlock soon became extremely popular with George's company because he was a great listener. He just loved to stand there as the soldiers chatted away to him or told him all their problems. In fact, he could listen for hours without moving a muscle. He was absolutely no trouble at all: the occasional pail of water and some porridge and a wagon to sleep under and he asked for nothing more.

But Lieutenant Brown discovered more of Fetlock's talents. This subaltern could actually ride so he took Fetlock to his favourite cafe in Ypres every night (this was early in 1918). Private James, the lieutenant's servant, had to go along as well because by closing time the officer was drunk. James had to be on hand to hoist him up on to Fetlock and lead him home.

One night Private James became inebriated himself and was not available when the lieutenant departed for Ypres. Brown had his usual skinful and then tottered out to Fetlock. Somehow, he managed to get aboard and Fetlock trotted off, taking the officer straight back to his billet, even waiting outside to make sure that Brown got into his bed safely. Subsequently, Private James was not required.

George was really saddened when the 24/Queen's moved on south in the spring of 1918 to the Mormal Forest area. Soon after their arrival Fetlock disappeared. He could have gone back to Ypres or he could have been stolen by another subaltern who needed transport home after an evening out.

Cats (& Birds) & Also a Mole

In 1915 refugee cats were used to keep down the mice population in the trenches. On Hill 60, south-east of Ypres, they were officially commissioned as 'Government Service Trench Cats, Mark VI', but after August, following a series of incidents in which nervous sentries blasted off into the night and invited retaliatory fire from Jerry, they were banned. But in no way did cats disappear from the battle zone; they just became unofficial. In June 1917 Private William Golightly (1/Northumberland Fusiliers) stared out through a peephole into no-man's-land and was surprised to see a pair of eyes staring back at him.

Other cats were solidly established as pets in the trenches. Christabel, the favourite of a company of the Argyll and Sutherland Highlanders, liked to sun herself on the parapet. One day, a German sniper mistook her for a Guardsman's bearskin. But the sharpshooter aimed for the 'Guardsman's' eyes with the result that only Christabel's backside was affected. Visitors were told the story, after which she was invited to show off her war wound. 'Show the officer your backside, Christabel,' instructed Lance-Corporal Bates, and Christabel obligingly lifted her tail to exhibit the damage. However, she packed up sunning herself on the parapet and now kipped exclusively on the fire step.

Sidney Rogerson of the 2/West Yorkshires heard a scuffling behind him under the parados (13 November 1917) and out popped a furry, fat mole. Rogerson held it for a few minutes and stroked it before letting it resume excavating. Rogerson wished he could dig as well as that – he could have built a really roomy dugout in no time at all.

Pigeons were used to convey messages from tanks to HQ. When a tank reached its target in the Battle of Passchendaele (September 1917), its commander prepared to send a message back to let command know. To encourage his pigeon he gave it seed-cake and a drop of whisky. But when the time came for the bird to depart, it refused to budge an inch. They slid the tank forward to shake it off the track but as it went forward the pigeon shifted backwards to maintain its position. It was obvious what the deal was: no more seed-cake, and especially no more whisky, and no more flying off with a message.

Private Scrivener (2/Queen Victoria Rifles) carried round a friendly bantam cock in a perforated biscuit tin (December 1914), but there was an unfortunate accident in 1915 when someone sat on it.

Skeff was a green parrot, the pet of the 4/Coldstream Guards. It enjoyed classical music and would sway from side to side to Strauss, and especially *Rosenkavalier*. It enjoyed sitting on men's shoulders. Indeed, if you scratched his ear he would lift his head and kindly deposit a pellet from his mouth into your ear. Alternatively, if you didn't scratch his ear he would let you have something from his other end.

Cows & Mules

Cows tended to feature on the Western Front on account of being a source of food and drink. However, it was unwise to underestimate their capabilities. The Munsters discovered this early in the war during the retreat from Mons. Owing to the breakdown of supply lines, the troops became interested in five cows proceeding sedately in front of them down a lane. It was a long and straight byway and the Munsters fancied their chances of waylaying at least one of the beasts. But suddenly, a gate appeared into a field and the leading cow slipped through it. The Munsters decided not to follow it because the Uhlans (German cavalry) were not far behind.

Another gate was reached and the next cow coolly entered it. Incredibly, this happened three more times and the Munsters were left staring up an empty lane. Now, did these five cows belong in five different fields? The Munsters couldn't hang around to find out.

There are a number of recorded instances of cows being maintained in trenches: Buffalo Bill's failed experiment was described in Chapter Three. The plan was to graze them at night and milk them during the day. Probably the idea fizzled out in 1915 because by that time there was little grass left in *la zone rouge*.

John Jackson, corporal of the guard at the Étaples training ground ('Bullring'), one night in the summer of 1916, challenged a dim shape that was moving quickly towards him. It refused to stop and Jackson was on the point of shooting it, whatever it was, when he recognised the 'cuddie' (donkey) from Angeline's (Lady Angela Forbes' nearby refreshment hut). Jackson gave it a prod in the flank and the cuddie accelerated sharply up the road. There were other sentries further along the road and Jackson was amused to hear each one shout, 'Halt! Who goes there?' Neddie must have built up a rare turn of speed by the time it reached the beach. It did go for the occasional swim but usually only during daylight hours.

A mule encountered by the 2/West Yorkshires at Oisemont was an interesting character. They were returning wearily from a spell in the Somme trenches. As they passed, the mule gave them a long, loud and hearty welcome. They could still hear it a mile away. Was it really bellowing 'hello' or was it uttering a requiem for the departed souls of tens of thousands of its species on the Western Front?

Baboon

Jackie the Baboon was the mascot of the 3/South African Infantry. An amiable personality, it always saluted the officers. Jackie was wounded twice and was able to place his paw gravely on his forehead to indicate to the doctor in what portion of his anatomy he had suffered. Happily, Jackie survived the war.

Jackie the Baboon, mascot of the 3rd South African Infantry.

Round-Up

'What's that, Sar'nt?' asked a Fusilier.

'That, me lad, is your bread ration.'

'Blimey, Sar'nt, I thought it were 'oly Communion.'

The 'conjuror' of the 2/RWF entertained his comrades with card tricks, during which he was also able to relieve them of what little money they had. He was the sort of bloke who sang *Somewhere the Sun is Shining* when it was hurtling down with rain in the trench. Elsewhere, at various venues, he sang obscene songs for 10 francs a night, plus liquid refreshment. On 10 July 1917 he 'found' a book of signed but blank hospital admittance forms and slid around the billets trying to flog them. Later, he was delivered unconscious into the local spud hole (guardroom) in a wheelbarrow. Usually, his comatose condition came as the result of heavy drinking, but on this occasion some person or persons unknown had beaten him up. The hospital admittance forms were nowhere to be seen and it seemed that he was in need of one.

In the hot summer of 1916 the Post Office Rifles were marching from Flanders to the Somme, quite a trek in extremely hot weather. Indeed, under this blazing sun two 'elderly' men died of heat-related conditions. The Rifles had nearly reached their destination, well-nigh knackered, hungry and well fed-up, when a general appeared and the officers got the Rifles into a shambles of a parade. Some of them could hardly stand up. But they had to listen to the general. 'Men,' he announced portentously, 'I have very great news for you.' The ex-postmen waited with baited breath – didn't they half. 'The Russians have won a great victory,' he concluded.

A rumble emerged from the ranks, and grew and grew in stature until the whole ragged lot of them were almost singing it out: 'F*** the Russians!'

In the Arras sector in June 1917 a platoon from the well-loved Durham Light Infantry removed an entire Nissen hut from over the heads of some slumbering Engineers. If you were short of a hut ...

A padre travelling by train to Boulogne was accompanied by a carriage full of subalterns and was boring them stupid (they would have preferred to have gone to sleep). He was mostly complaining about lax sexual morality on the Western Front. 'That hospital in Boulogne, the Venereal Diseases Hospital,' he told them, 'is absolutely crammed with officers and men who have sinned.'

A 2nd lieutenant couldn't resist this opportunity. 'Oh yes, padre,' he said brightly, 'the patients now have to fall in by companies, battalions, regiments and brigades. Generals with syphilis on the right of the line; chaplains with gonorrhoea on the left. The sheep and the goats!'

The Battle of the Somme was in full swing in July 1916 and Lieutenant-General Sir Ivor Maxse, a corps commander, addressed thousands of troops during a Sunday parade with lavish patriotic fervour. Men at the back could afford to laugh with impunity. 'It's a load of jelly-bellied flag-flapping!' was the loud opinion of one sergeant.

Mackenzie was the medical officer of the 25/King's Royal Rifles and survived all the major battles of the war. Habitually he forgot to shave, wash, brush his hair and had a wild, tramp-like appearance. He had long ago lost his own cap and wore one which he had found and was several sizes too small for him. He had lost most of his buttons and his 'uniform' was mainly held together by string. Mackenzie spent many hours searching for souvenirs in no-man's-land – he favoured fuses and German helmets. One day he wandered for several miles and then sat on top of a mound watching an artillery battery at work. 'Oh, I say, good shot,' he would cry out from time to time.

A sergeant came over and arrested him at gunpoint. Mackenzie's CO had to send someone over to release him – not for the first time. On one trip home on leave the good doctor managed to terrify his neighbours in Teddington by throwing a blazing primus stove out of an upstairs window. They thought they were being attacked by a Zeppelin. Later that week his newborn baby was nowhere to be seen and the neighbours' consensus was that Mackenzie, long considered by them as mad, had got rid of the child. Indeed, one person claimed to have seen Mackenzie creeping out at night with a large, black bag slung over his shoulder. Inside it, the witness swore, something was squirming.

The truth was that he had gone down to the Thames to drown some unwanted kittens. He had taken his little boy down to his mother in Hastings in order to get some sleep.

On another leave he was arrested by police after getting into a fight with a swan. On yet another occasion he was coming home on a train in England when his travelling companions complained about the pong emanating from his bag. Shrugging, he dragged out the hand he had cut from a Jerry corpse and slung it out of the window. In short, Mackenzie was truly nuts, but he also happened to be the local trench expert on where the next shell would fall and was able to maintain his popularity on account of this ability. Soldiers tended to keep him company.

'Pferfies' were a solid feature of everyday life on the Western Front. This was the popular name for rumours. These were usually delivered – as 'officials', of course – in latrine, cookhouse or ration dump, etc. The name may have originated from 'Murphy', since it was widely believed that most rumours were started by Irishmen.

It was actually Private Frank Honeywood of the ANZACs who started many of them – on purpose to see in what form they came back to him. For instance, late in 1916 he whispered to someone sitting in the karsy with him that 'the Russian bear was training large bodies of men in the use of a secret weapon'. Three weeks later, again sitting in the karsy, he was told that 'the Russians were training a brigade of bears to fight with razor blades attached to their paws'.

Lieutenant-Colonel Osburn, who held various commands in field medical units, wrote a fascinating account of his experiences in his book *Unwilling Passenger*. He had an idea for a war memorial. He believed it should be a statue of a Tommy lying face down in a latrine, his skull crushed by a flying latrine bucket (full or empty. he did not specify).

The 4/Coldstream Guards, when marching from the bloody picnic of the Somme, passed a little old lady pushing some belongings in a wheelbarrow. It was the first civilian the Guards had seen for two months: they were very pleased to see her. ''Ullo, Grandma,' one of them called over cheerfully. 'Good to see you, Grandma. Three cheers for Grandma!'

The responses down the line were deafening: ''Ullo, Grandma! Three cheers for Grandma! Hip, hip, hooray! Hip, hip, hooray! Hip, hip, hooray!'

The old girl stood there waving and grinning (toothlessly) for fifteen minutes as the whole battalion trudged by. ''Ullo, Grandma. Three cheers for Grandma! Hip, hip, hooray! Hip, hip, hooray! Hip, hip, hooray!'

It's not a bad way to say cheerio to Tommy.

Bibliography

Arthur, Max, *Forgotten Voices of the Great War*, London, 2002

Ashworth, Tony, *Trench Warfare 1914–1918: the Live and Let Live System*, London, 1980

Bairnsfather, Bruce, *Bullets and Billets*, London, 1916

Barton, Peter (ed.), *Beneath Flanders Fields, The Tunnellers' War 1914–18*, Stroud, 2007

Behrend, Arthur, *As from Kemmel Hill*, London, 1963

The Best 500 Cockney War Stories, Stroud, 2009

Bickersteth, Ella, *The Bickersteth Diaries 1914–1918*, London, 1995

Bilton, David, *The Trench: the Full Story of the 1st Hull Pals*, Barnsley, 2002

Blacker, C.P., *Have you Forgotten London Yet?*, London, 2000

Brophy, John & Partridge, Eric, *Dictionary of Tommies' Songs and Slang 1914–18*, Barnsley, 2008

Brown, Malcolm, *1914: The Men Who Went to War*, London, 2005

Bruckshaw, Horace, *The Diaries of Pte. Horace Bruckshaw 1915–1916*, London, 1979

Bryant, Mark, *World War I Cartoons*, London, 2006

Campbell, P.J., *In the Cannon's Mouth*, London, 1979

Carr, William, *A Time to Leave the Ploughshares: a Gunner Remembers*, London, 1985

Carrington, Charles, *Soldier from the War Returning*, Barnsley, 2006

Congreve, Billy, *Armageddon Road: A VC's Diary, 1914–1916*, London, 1982

Coppard, George, *With a Machine Gun to Cambrai*, London, 1980

Craster, J., *Fifteen Rounds a Minute*, London, 1976

Eberle, V.F., *My Sapper Venture*, London, 1973

Edmonds, Charles, *A Subaltern's War*, London, 1929

'Ex-Private X', *War is War*, London, 1930

Feilding, Rowland, *War Letters to a Wife: France and Flanders 1915–1919*, London, 1929

French, Anthony, *Gone for a Soldier*, Kineton, 1972

Fussell, Paul, *The Great War and Modern Memory*, New York & London, 1975

Glubb, John, *Into Battle: A Soldier's Diary of the Great War*, London, 1977

Graham, Stephen, *A Private in the Guards*, London, 1928

Graves, Robert, *Goodbye to All That: An Autobiography*, Oxford, 1995

Greenwell, Graham, H., *An Infant in Arms: Letters of a Company Officer 1914–1918*, London, 1972

Groom, Winston, *A Storm in Flanders: Triumph and Tragedy on the Western Front*, London, 2002

Harris, Ruth-Elwin, *Billie: the Nevill Letters 1914–1916*, London, 1991

Hawkings, Frank, *From Ypres to Cambrai: The Diary of an Infantryman 1914–1919*, Morley (Yorkshire), 1974

Hay, Ian, *The First Hundred Thousand*, Edinburgh & London, 1915

Holmes, Richard, *The Western Front*, London, 2001

———, *Shots from the Front: The British Soldier 1914–1918*, London, 2008

Holt, Tonie & Valmai, *In Search of a Better 'Ole: A Biography of Captain Bruce Bairnsfather*, Barnsley, 2001

Jackson, John, *Private 12768: Memoir of a Tommy*, Stroud, 2005

Livermore, Bernard, *Long 'Un – A Damn Bad Soldier*, Batley, 1974

Livingstone, Thomas, *Tommy's War: a First World War Diary 1913–18*, London, 2008

Lynch, E.P.F., *Somme Mud: The Experiences of an Infantryman in France 1916–1919*, London, 2006

MacArthur, Brian, *For King and Country: Voices from the First World War*, London, 2008

Macdonald, Lyn, *1914–1918: Voices and Images of the Great War*, London, 1991

BIBLIOGRAPHY

Mottram, R.H., *Three Personal Records of the War*, London, 1929

Moynihan, Michael, *Greater Love: Letters Home 1914–1918*, London, 1980

Munson, James (ed.), *Echoes of the Great War: The Diary of the Reverend Andrew Clark 1914–1919*, Oxford, 1985

Nicholls, Jonathan, *Cheerful Sacrifice: The Battle of Arras 1917*, London, 1990

Ogle, Henry, *The Fateful Battle Line*, Barnsley, 1993

Parker, Ernest, *Into Battle 1914–1918*, London, 1964

Read, I.L., *Of Those we Loved*, Bishop Auckland, 1994

Reith, John, *Wearing Spurs*, London, 1966

Richards, Frank, *Old Soldiers Never Die*, London, 1933

Rogerson, Sidney, *Twelve Days of the Somme: A Memoir of the Trenches, 1916*, London, 2006

Simpson, Andy, *Hot Blood and Cold Steel*, Staplehurst, 2002

Slack, C.M., *Grandfather's Adventures in the Great War 1914–1918*, Ilfracombe, 1977

Spicer, Lancelot Dykes, *Letters from France 1915–1918*, London, 1979

Terraine, John, *General Jack's Diary, 1914–1918*, London, 2000

Tyndale-Biscoe, Julian, *Gunner Subaltern 1914–1918*, London, 1971

Van Emden, Richard, *Britain's Last Tommies*, Barnsley, 2005

——, *The Trench: Experiencing Life on the Front Line, 1916*, London, 2002

Vansittart, Peter, *Voices from the Great War*, London, 1998

Vaughan, Edwin Campion, *Some Desperate Glory: The Diary of a Young Officer 1917*, London, 1981

Walsh, Michael, *Brothers in War*, London, 2007

Weeks, Alan, *Tea, Rum and Fags: Sustaining Tommy 1914–1918*, Stroud, 2009

Weeks, George, unpublished memoirs of the Great War

Weintraub, Stanley, *Silent Night*, London, 2001

The Wipers Times: The complete series of the famous wartime trench newspaper, London, 2006

Young, Derek, *Scottish Voices from the Great War*, Stroud, 2006

Index

INDEX